REAL DISCIPLESHIP

REAL
DISCIPLESHIP

How to Follow Jesus
His Way—Not Ours

FR. JEFFREY KIRBY

Catholic
Answers
Press

Published by Catholic Answers, Inc.
2020 Gillespie Way
El Cajon, California 92020
1-888-291-8000 orders
619-387-0042 fax
catholic.com

Printed in the United States of America

Cover and interior design by Claudine Mansour Design

978-1-68357-353-1
978-1-68357-354-8 Kindle
978-1-68357-355-5 ePub

*In Gratitude for the Witness of
the Vaughan Family
Deacon Jason, Audrey, and Dominic*

CONTENTS

INTRODUCTION

Throughout my priestly ministry, I have always encouraged people to read the Bible. At a time when God, his revelation, and sacred teachings are distorted and redefined, it is a safe first practice to lead people to the Bible. By reading it, a person encounters a living word. He sees and hears God on his own terms, from his own deeds and words. Although more teaching will be needed, this initial practice of reading the Bible can dispel false images, correct wayward views, and challenge distorted definitions and flawed understandings of divine realities.

When I encourage people to read the Bible, I direct them to one of the four Gospel books, in which we come face to face with Jesus Christ, the Word made flesh and our anointed Savior. In the Gospels, counterfeit versions of the Christ are exposed and hung out to dry. The darkness of deception is scattered, and shadows are filled with light. We see Jesus Christ for who he is—not what our fallen hearts or our tainted culture want him to be. We hear firsthand the summons to follow him and be his disciples. There is no room for compromise or accommodation. The Lord Jesus speaks, and we are invited to listen. He summons, and we are called to follow.

These encouragements to read the Bible are often ignored, but there also graced moments when people respond. They pick up their Bibles, dust them off, and begin reading one of the Gospel books.

On one such occasion, an older woman accepted the invitation and decided to read one of the Gospels. It convicted her so profoundly that she read the other three. After completing all four, she reached out and asked to meet with me. I was happy to comply and was eager to hear what the Holy Spirit was doing in her heart.

As we met, I sensed she was nervous. In an attempt to make her comfortable, I made some small talk. After a few passing questions, the older woman looked me dead in the eyes and said, "Okay, let's get to it!"

"I agree," I responded. "How did the reading of the Gospel books go? Were you able to see the Lord Jesus for who he is?"

"Father," the woman replied, "I'm in my seventies. I've been Catholic my whole life. I went through Catholic schools. I raised my children Catholic. And . . . well, it was very unsettling to read the Gospel books. I'm not sure why you want us to do that."

"Well, as Christians we should know as much as we can about the Lord Jesus. By reading the Bible, especially the Gospels, we can know more about it. Since the Bible is a living word, the Lord Jesus is actually present to us when we read the Bible. He is accompanying us, loving us, and teaching us. That's why I encourage us to read the Bible. Does that make sense?"

"Father," she replied, I just didn't realize everything he said, or the things he wants us to do. There were times when Jesus just seemed rude. He was pushy. I'm sure I heard all of this before, but is he for real?" And then looking at a list she composed, the woman continued, "Go the extra mile when someone already forces you to go one, forgive seventy-seven times, carry a cross, turn the other cheek when someone hits you? . . . and there's more? Is Jesus serious?!"

"Yes, the Lord Jesus is dead serious. Did you notice that he is describing his own life? He is paraphrasing his life while calling us to live the same way. This is what he means when he summons us to *follow* him. The Lord Jesus is living a very different, countercultural way of life for his time, as well as for our own. Our fallenness as human beings is the same in every age. Our self-focus and selfishness are the same in every age. Cultures change, technologies are developed, times are different, but our fallen nature remains the same. But the Lord Jesus shows us a new and different way. He breaks the cycles of fallenness and sin and offers us the path of love and eternal life. This is the way we are called to follow as Christians. This is the way we accept when we choose to follow the Lord Jesus: to be his *disciple*."

Throughout my comments, the woman was visibly uneasy. As she squirmed in her seat, she was ready to respond. "Well, that's what bothers me the most. I'm reading about Jesus, and what he asked of the people when he was alive. And, honestly, Father, I'm scared because *if I were alive when Jesus was preaching all this stuff, I don't think I would have followed him.*"

"Well, thanks be to God! You are realizing the real demands of what it means to be a disciple of the Lord Jesus! And the Lord doesn't just preach those things for people 2,000 years ago. He continues to preach his way to us today. And you are being very transparent with your answer to his call. This is good news! If we're all honest, there are times in which we all struggle with one or some of the commands of the Lord Jesus, but it is precisely our openness that allows his grace to work in us and to do in us what we didn't think possible.

"The Holy Spirit can transform doubters, weaklings, and procrastinators," I continued, "but he cannot transform *deceivers*. The Holy Spirit can work with honesty, even honest doubts and fears, but he cannot work with half-truths, adulterated truth, or raw lies. The Holy Spirit cannot work with liars, but he can *always* work with repentant sinners. So, don't be afraid of your integrity. It will be the means by which God blesses and works through you."

"Oh, Father, thank you. This is very encouraging. I thought I was a goner. But I'm still not sure about some of the things the Lord is asking of me."

"We're all works in progress. The fact that you know what discipleship means and that you want to live up to its calling is a good start. Keep praying for the graces of conversion and keep doing all that the Lord asks of you as best you can."

The woman had walked into my office with uncertainty and fear. She now left my office with faith and a conviction to follow the Lord Jesus. She left my office a *disciple*.

A Universal Call to Discipleship and Holiness

The call of the Lord Jesus is for everyone. There is no elitism in the invitation to accept the gospel. Every man and every woman of every vocation is called to be a disciple of the Lord Jesus and to pursue his universal call to holiness.

At certain regrettable points in the spiritual tradition of the Church, the demands of discipleship were often carved out and applied only to those in holy orders or religious life, leaving discipleship for the laity—the vast majority of the Church—minimized. Too many Christians didn't know the full extent of what the Lord was asking of his disciples. They didn't know that they, too, in *everything* they said and did, were called to take up the cross and faithfully follow the Lord Jesus.

Thanks be to God, in our time, the universal call to holiness is back in the center of the Church's spiritual life, where it belongs. The Church once again announces that every person is called to follow Jesus. Every baptized disciple is called to the rigors and hardships, joys and triumphs, of a life completely devoted to the Lord. As the Second Vatican Council put it,

> Thus it is evident to everyone, that all the faithful of Christ of whatever rank or status, are called to the fullness of the Christian life and to the perfection of charity . . . In order that the faithful may reach this perfection, they must use their strength accordingly as they have received it, as a gift from Christ. They must follow in his footsteps and conform themselves to his image seeking the will of the Father in all things. They must devote themselves with all their being to the glory of God and the service of their neighbor. In this way, the holiness of the People of God will grow into an abundant harvest of good, as is admirably shown by the life of so many saints in Church history" (*Lumen Gentium* 40).

The Standard of the Cross

In our fallen world, humanity seems always ready to define Christian discipleship without the cross. Marked with a sinful self-absorption, we are eager to strip the cross of its power (1 Cor. 1:17) and create our own version of what it means to follow the way of the Lord.

The cross, however, is the *standard of discipleship*. It lies at the very heart of the invitation of the Lord Jesus to follow him:

> Then Jesus told his disciples, "If anyone would come after me, let him deny himself and take up his cross and follow me. For whoever would save his life will lose it, but whoever loses his life for my sake will find it. For what will it profit a man if he gains the whole world and forfeits his soul? Or what shall a man give in return for his soul?" (Matt. 16:24–26).

Many disciples are born into the Faith. The Church offers infant baptism with the understanding that a post-baptismal family-oriented catechumenate will happen at home. Parents and godparents promise before God and the Church that they will ensure the Christian formation of the children entrusted to them. Regrettably, though, often this ongoing formation does not occur or is deficient. As such, countless Christians have incomplete or wayward understandings of what it means to be a disciple of Jesus Christ. And these understandings seldom include the cross.

In place of the cross are bizarre self-styled identities of Jesus and self-composed versions of the gospel. The wood of the cross is replaced by spiritual Styrofoam, and self-oblation by self-indulgence. The relativism and sentimentalism of contemporary Western culture deplete the radical nature of what it means to be a disciple of the God-Man. In this age, even lifelong Catholic Christians never learn about the outpouring of self that goes with the vocation of being a disciple of the Lord Jesus. Or worse: they actively resist, in word and deed, the connection between discipleship and the cross.

But if there is no cross, there is no discipleship. Any claims of discipleship that ignore or diminish the cross are frauds.

The "Good-Enough" Gospel

Many Catholics today have been taught to be content with a minimal form of discipleship. They were taught that sitting through a weekly Mass is "good enough." Some think it's good enough just to say a few prayers at night and read a little bit of the Bible. Others think it's good enough merely to be kind to others, smile, and not cause any trouble. In each of these examples, and others like them, there is no mention of God, Jesus Christ, the cross, grace, or eternal life.

Real discipleship smashes the "good enough" gospel. The gospel of Jesus Christ shatters the sell-out gospels of our day. And the authentic disciple of the Lord Jesus, who lives selflessly for him and his gospel, exposes the counterfeit Christianity of our times.

When those with depreciated notions of discipleship begin to hear of the full demands of discipleship or read the Gospel books for the first time, and encounter the summons to the cross or see the witness of another who is truly following the way of the Lord, they are shocked, unsettled, and dismayed. They honestly don't know how to reconcile their faux versions of discipleship with real discipleship. In such moments, either "good enough" will kick in and they'll lie to themselves that they're doing well in *their religion*, or they will continue to ask questions and ultimately be led to an authentic relationship with Jesus Christ and his Church.

The "good enough" gospel is fed by false understandings of the living God and his Son, Jesus Christ. It builds upon a lack of knowledge of the Christ's teachings and the way of life to which he calls us. Relying on idolatry, compromise, relativism, and half-measures, the "good enough" gospel relishes accommodation, comfort, and a radical form of autonomy or self-will.

The Pet Deity

As children, my siblings and I always had pets around. Our house was always a house of dogs. It's a joy now to see my nieces, nephews, and grandnieces have dogs in their lives as they grow up. As they interact with their pets, they learn to tell them what they want or don't want them to do. If the pets show that they need something, through their non-verbal communication, they can be given attention and care, or can be ignored or dismissed. But the pets can't talk back. They can't give *us* commands. When well trained, the pets just do what they're told.

The pets are precisely that: pets. They are meant to stay in their lane and contribute to our well-being. They make us feel good, warm, protected, and . . . they do whatever we want, or they get disciplined or discarded. When lived virtuously, this is a good state of affairs when dealing with our canine companions or other pets.

There is a fundamental problem, however, when we treat God like a pet. Too often we expect that God, infinitely perfect and blessed in himself, the Ancient of Days and the Beginning and End of all things, will domesticate himself for us. We expect the good feelings, the warmth and protection, but he can make no commands or demands. This pet deity must stay in the lane that we have given him. God has no place to tell *us* how to live, worship, love, or follow him. He is on our leash, and he will submit to us. We have become like gods. Our whims have become the gospel. Our desires and our will to power have become our perverse form of discipleship.

When God becomes our pet, we shouldn't be surprised to hear that idolatry is always barking at the door.

The Idolatrous "My Jesus"

Biblically, an *idol* is anything to which we give the adoration and submission that are due to God alone. The ancient world worshipped personal idols, such as Zeus and Athena. Our contemporary world struggles with more spiritual idols, idols that are more discreet and seductive, such as pleasure, money, and power. Just as, in the early centuries after Christ, ancient peoples tried to retain their idolatry and impose it upon the gospel, leading to Christological heresies such as Docetism and Arianism, so contemporary peoples persist in their idolatry and seek to inflict it upon the gospel, leading to false gospels of hedonism, materialism, and utilitarianism. All these modern heresies contain grave misconceptions about discipleship and what it means to adore and submit to the living God.

Whenever an idol—whatever it might be—becomes a template for discipleship, a false messiah is crowned, a perverse gospel is defended, and a deviant discipleship is created. Such messiahs, gospels, and notions of discipleship are diametrically opposed to the Lord Jesus Christ, as he is known with surety from history and divine revelation, from his saving gospel, and from the way of discipleship that he offers to us.

One expression of such idolatry is when people speak of "my Jesus." In this context, the term is not being used in a devotional way, to express affection to the Lord, but rather as an assertion of a self-created, self-defined Jesus. In this way, the expression "my Jesus" is similar in spirit to the popular term "my truth." In such a way, what sounds like devotion is actually rebellion against the real Jesus Christ of history and divine revelation. The fanciful claim of "my Jesus," wrapped in relativism, egoism, and sentimentalism, asserts that simply because a person thinks, wants, or feels that the Lord Jesus should be a certain way, he therefore is. People with their personal Jesus presume to change the real, perfect identity of Jesus Christ and the unchanging truth of his teachings to suit their own preferences and likings.

Real discipleship, however, means accepting Jesus Christ as he is truly known from history and divine revelation. Discipleship is dying to ourselves, and that includes dying to what we *want* the Lord Jesus to be or to teach. It means surrendering to Jesus Christ as "the Way, the Truth, and the Life" (John 14:6). This is the task, challenge, and arduous journey of real discipleship.

The Witness of the Early Church

The demands of real discipleship can be overwhelming, as the older woman herself remarked in the previous story: "If I were alive when Jesus was preaching all this stuff, I don't think I would have followed him." The demands, however, can be faithfully met through the grace of the sacraments and the witness, encouragement, and spiritual solidarity of other believers, both living and dead.

Of the countless fellow believers that we have throughout the world today, and throughout the Church's long and beautiful history, no group of Christians can compete or rival with the heroic lives and witness of our early Church fathers and mothers.

From the public ministry of the Lord Jesus, there were men and women who heard him preach and chose to follow him. They saw in Jesus of Nazareth the long-awaited Messiah and they came to know and believe that he was the Son of God, as St. Peter himself exclaims: "Lord, to whom can we go? You have the words of eternal life. We have come to believe and know that you are the Holy One of God" (John 6:68–69). The early disciples heard the challenge of the cross, understood the demands of a death to themselves and their fallenness, and were eager to do whatever the Lord Jesus asked, so as to be with him, to follow his path of love, and to work out their eternal salvation by the workings of his grace.

As recounted in the four Gospel books, the Acts of the Apostles, and in various portions of the apostolic letters of the New Testament, the early disciples of the Lord Jesus believed, or came to believe, in one, true God and in his Son, Jesus Christ. They understood the gospel as the definitive and life-saving message of eternal life. The early disciples recognized the way of the Lord Jesus as the way of the cross and as the only sure way to salvation. They realized that the Lord Jesus, once he ascended into heaven, would return again—and they pined for his return. The first Christians saw the fragility of salvation, the urgency of the message given to them, the power of authentic freedom, and the fullness of what it means to be loved and to love.

The entire way of life of the first Christians and their descendants was marked by these clear, objective truths. There was no room for illusions or any privatization of what the Lord Jesus lived and taught. It was about truth.

It was about love. It was about acknowledging the real identity of Jesus Christ and the integrity of taking up the call to follow him as his disciples. Such a worldview, and the culture that flowed from it, was the impetus behind the aggressive efforts to evangelize all peoples. It was the clarity that invigorated our early theologians and the source of the stamina that galvanized the strength of our early martyrs.

Such an environment gave birth to a robust and compelling notion of real discipleship, which led to a vibrant, dynamic Church in the midst of the world. With this in mind, we can turn to the early Church as a guide and model for us as we seek to answer and receive clarification on what it means to be a disciple of the Lord Jesus and to faithfully follow his way today.

Why This Book?

This book is written out of a desire to renew, spell out, and reinvigorate our contemporary notions of real discipleship. In the West today, it has become disturbingly apparent that there is an urgent need to reform and restore the understanding of Christian discipleship within the firm convictions of one God, one saving Lord, one life-giving cross, and one definitive gospel. This book will cover these pressing themes, and others relating to them.

Chapter one covers the central tenet of the Judeo-Christian tradition: namely, there is one God. In contrast to the One-of-Many argument, the chapter will show that there is only one true God and his Son, Jesus Christ. The singularity of the lordship of Jesus Christ will be explored and explained in relation to real discipleship.

Chapter two dives into the efforts to turn the one gospel into a nice, fanciful story. The chapter will show the historical reality of the public ministry of Jesus Christ and his gospel. It will provide a broad summary of the demands and expectations of the gospel within real discipleship.

Chapter three explores the one way of the Lord Jesus and its challenges and rewards. It builds upon the first two chapters and points us to the fourth. It seeks to provide a holistic summary of what it means to follow the way of the Lord. It exposes the inclination to compromise and the deception of relativism and sentimentalism in circumventing the commands of the Lord Jesus.

Chapter four plunges into the beauty and power of the paschal mystery and the eucharistic sacrifice. The many efforts to turn the sacrifice into a meal or something on the merely human level will be dissected and the reality of the holy sacrifice given to us by Jesus Christ will be explained and applied to our discipleship.

The book concludes with a review of our call to be real disciples of Jesus Christ and to unconditionally and joyfully surrender to his lordship.

The Structure of This Book

After this introduction, each chapter of the book provides teachings on a false view of some essential component of real discipleship. It compares the false view against an authentic view of real discipleship. After the chapter's teachings, there will be a section on applying them to our lives, containing the following:

Declarations of Discipleship

A few brief statements of belief are offered, to assist you in making an immediate application of the different points to your own discipleship.

Examination of Conscience

Each chapter provides a series of questions meant to help you identify aspects of the respective form of false discipleship in your own heart and in our society.

Key points

These assist you in reviewing the principal lessons of the chapter and provide you with a brief summary of points to share with others.

Devotional Exercise

In each chapter I will included proposed prayers and devotions to help you keep false discipleship away from your own heart and home and cultivate real discipleship.

———

With the struggle of redefined and erroneous notions of discipleship before us, we are in great need of a thorough study of the true and biblical notions of real discipleship.

It is my hope that this book will contribute to this overall mission, and that it might assist you in some way to bring about a deepening of true discipleship in your own heart.

And so, let's begin!

We pray:

> Put false ways far from me;
>   and graciously teach me your law.
> I have chosen the way of faithfulness;
>   I set your ordinances before me.
> I cling to your decrees, O Lord;
>   Let me not be put to shame.
> I run the way of your commandments,
>   for you enlarge my understanding.

—PSALM 119:29–32

CHAPTER ONE

THE ONE LORD, NOT ONE-OF-MANY

For who is God except the Lord?
  And who is a rock besides our God?—
the God who girded me with strength,
  and made my way safe.

—PSALM 18:31–32

Some time ago, I was at an event at a public venue. The Roman collar naturally attracts people and so I wasn't surprised when a fellow participant made his way toward me and started a conversation. The gentleman asked me if I was a Catholic priest. I responded in the affirmative and he seemed pleased, saying to me, "Wonderful! I have a great admiration for the teachings of Jesus Christ."

It was an attempt at graciousness, but I always cringe when I hear such comments because of the unintentional condescension that usually follows. Such statements put a person's personal assent over divine teaching. The man's "admiration" was the emphasis, not the "teachings of Jesus Christ." Such an approach relegates eternal truth to personal preferences and pleasure. Despite being overtures of supposed goodwill, such comments are offensive to the dignity and objectivity of sacred teachings.

The sequence of the conversation was, therefore, very predictable.

I smiled and sought to kindly nod as the man attempted to show some type of esteem for the religious teacher of some priest he just met. And true to form, the gentleman continued, saying, "Yes, I value the spiritual wisdom of all religious traditions. There's a beauty in the thoughts of Buddha, the prayers of Hinduism, the moral teachings of Mohammed, and the gospel of mercy given by Jesus Christ."

Wallowing in his own enlightenment, the man was actually patronizing the "religious traditions" that he was claiming to respect. The offense of syncretism is, indeed, often veiled under a false claim of admiration.

After the gentleman made his comments, I responded quietly, "It's wonderful that you are taking your soul and its nourishment so seriously. It's good to seek wisdom. My question, however, is how you reconcile the claims of Jesus Christ with your personal pantheon of spiritual wisdom."

The gentleman seemed confused. He tilted his head a bit, non-verbally inquiring as to what I was asking him. And so, I continued, "Within your manicured collection of spiritual traditions, there is one that is not like the others. Unlike Buddha, or Mohammed, or the authors of the *Upanishads*, Jesus Christ claimed to be God. He made a radically distinct claim that demands either acceptance or rejection. Good religious leaders don't claim to be a god if they're not. And so, Jesus Christ is either God or he is the worst of all so-called religious leaders and the most vile and deceptive of human beings."

I paused and then continued, "There is no clumping Jesus Christ with revered religious leaders and teachers of wisdom. He is understood within his own context, and such a context demands either complete assent or harsh rejection. There is no chorus with Jesus Christ. He is a sole cantor, and we have to decide whether his song is one of truth or one of treachery. If you're intellectually honest, you have to make a decision."

The man's face fell while I was speaking, and his eyes began to scan the room for other conversation partners. Regrettably, as I concluded my comments, he gave a forced smile and our discussion ended. I was saddened to see him walk away. I had hoped to continue the conversation, but he wasn't interested. I pray that some of the seeds of truth from our conversation may yet grow within him and lead him to a greater understanding of the Lord Jesus.

The Old and New Pantheon

In classical times, the *pantheon* was a collection of the deities. Meaning "all the gods," a pantheon served as an important public summary of who the gods were, especially as foreign and other new deities were added to a city-state's civic life. The pantheon was the focal point of religious and cultural meaning. In our times, we can use the word to refer to a collection of artificial things that have been given divine status. For example, the gentleman above was actually only giving homage to himself, not to any assumed deity. He was selecting, adjusting, interpreting, and choosing how to apply random spiritual wisdom to his own life, and so was only worshipping his own intellect and power to decide what is or is not wisdom or truth.

Other pantheons in our age include money and the market, political parties and intrigue, social ideologies, cultural fashions, human affection, respectability, creature comforts, and personal autonomy. The modern pantheon is a whirlwind of idols, a precious collection of personal preferences, sentiments, ambitions, and movements of the heart. However loose and oddly conjoined they might be, modern people consider their pantheons untouchable and fiercely protect them. Even when they have nothing to do with any notion of deity or divinity, but only the projected ambition and desire of our fallen human hearts, pantheons are always considered sacred.

The relativists of today do not like to be called out. They will guard their pantheons. The syncretists of our day, thinking they can mix and match religious ideas as they wish, do not like being reminded of the particularity of Jesus Christ. The egalitarians of our age cannot accept a claim of divinity. Contemporary man cannot fathom the reality of anything in his pantheon bowing to one true God, and he cannot even begin to remotely accept that such a God would become human and dwell among us.

Indeed, the claims of one true God and one sole mediator between God and men rock humanity's spiritual and religious horizon. Such claims are as shocking today as they were in bygone eras that first heard their proclamation. Today, the faith of Father Abraham and the faith of Jesus Christ are as jaw-dropping and startling to humanity as they were when they were revealed in their day.

One God? One mediator? This sounds like crazy talk to the contemporary Western serf, who thinks he is free and independent but who is actually spiritually displaced and enslaved to a new polytheism and a dictatorship of relativism.

Do we see the connection between old paganism and an aggressive new form of paganism? As Christian believers, have we forgotten the radical novelty and newness of believing and proclaiming one God and one Mediator? In our interactions in society, do we respond to any attempts to clump Jesus Christ into some hodgepodge creation of contemporary pantheons?

One God, Living and True

In all my years of priestly ministry and homiletics, I've preached on every imaginable topic. If it's happening in our society and the People of God must navigate it, then I'm going to preach about it. There have been homilies on abortion, so-called gay marriage, transgenderism, immigration, gender equality, and the list go on. To my great sorrow, there have been times when people have walked out on a challenging homily.

On one such occasion, years ago, I was doing a homily series on the commandments. The first homily was on the first commandment, and I stressed that there is one God and that he alone must be worshipped. Such a teaching should not be shocking or off-putting to any Christian. It is the bedrock of the revelations given to us by the true and living God. He announced himself to our father Abraham:

> When Abram was ninety-nine years old, the Lord appeared to Abram, and said to him, "I am God Almighty; walk before me, and be blameless. And I will make my covenant between me and you, and will make you exceedingly numerous" (Gen. 17:1).

And later he again revealed himself to his servant Moses, after liberating his people from slavery in Egypt:

> Then God spoke all these words: "I am the Lord your God, who brought you out of the land of Egypt, out of the house of slavery; you shall have no other gods before me. You shall not make for yourself an idol, whether in the form of anything that is in heaven above, or that is on the earth beneath, or that is in the water under the earth. You shall not bow down to them or worship them; for I the Lord your God am a jealous God, punishing children for the iniquity of parents, to the third and the fourth generation of those who reject me, but showing steadfast love to the thousandth generation of those who love me and keep my commandments" (Exod. 20:1–6).

If there was any confusion, God gave his people the *Shema*. This daily prayer would become the highest prayer of God's people in the Old Covenant:

> Hear, O Israel: The Lord is our God, the Lord alone. You shall love the Lord your God with all your heart, and with all your soul, and with all your might. Keep these words that I am commanding you today in your heart (Deut. 6:4–6).

The living God is very clear. There's no wiggle room. He has revealed himself to us and he calls us to draw close to him.

It was unsettling, therefore, that of all the homilies I have preached, and of all the controversial issues I have addressed, the homily I preached on the first commandment—on the oneness of God—is the *one that most people have walked out on*. The core teaching of one God provoked people enough to get up and walk out of Mass!

This response is a regrettable retrieval of an ancient past. As God's people journeyed with him through the covenants of the Old Testament, they were constantly learning, being disciplined, and called back to the worship of the one, true, and ever-living God. For Israel constantly sought other gods; it worshipped idols, compromised revelation, persecuted the messengers of God, and opened its doors to the influences and cultures of paganistic peoples.

Among the gentile nations, the claims of Israel seemed preposterous. The assertion that there is only one God and that he is the God of Israel was considered arrogant and pompous. How could any one people claim such a thing? And yet, in its moments of faithfulness, God's people made just such a bold proclamation, and they suffered for it.

In today's world, we see a return of those charges of hubris. The fallen world, and especially Western civilization, considers it offensive and even a bully tactic to claim that there is just one God. A civilization poisoned by relativism, sentimentalism, and syncretism abhors such assertions. God must be whatever we want him (or her, or it) to be. He is our creation, our personal Higher Power , and he will adjust to our whims.

The early Church, born from the Old Covenant and hailed as "the Israel of God" (Gal. 6:16), carried on the proclamation of God's people: there is only one God, living and true! The absolute monotheism of the Old Covenant was the foundation of the Church's understanding of the Holy Trinity and the divinity of Jesus Christ.

Using the faith and witness of Father Abraham, the Lord Jesus was clear on his oneness with the Father:

> They answered him, "Abraham is our father." Jesus said to them, "If you were Abraham's children, you would be doing what Abraham did, but now you are trying to kill me, a man who has told you the truth that I heard from God. This is not what Abraham did. You are indeed doing what your father does." They said to him, "We are not illegitimate children; we have one father, God himself." Jesus said to them, "If God were your Father, you would love me, for I came from God and now I am here. I did not come on my own, but he sent me. Why do you not understand what I say? It is because you cannot accept my word.
>
> "Very truly, I tell you, whoever keeps my word will never see death." The Jews said to him, "Now we know that you have a demon. Abraham died, and so did the prophets; yet you say, 'Whoever keeps my word will never taste death.' Are you greater than our father Abraham, who died? The prophets also died. Who do you claim to be?" Jesus answered, "If I glorify myself, my glory is nothing. It is my Father who glorifies me, he of whom you say, 'He is our God,' though you do not know him. But I know him; if I would say that I do not know him, I would be a liar like you. But I do know him and I keep his word. Your ancestor Abraham rejoiced that he would see my day; he saw it and was glad." Then the Jews said to him, "You

are not yet fifty years old, and have you seen Abraham?" Jesus said to them, "Very truly, I tell you, before Abraham was, I am" (John 8:39–43; 51–58).

As God continued to reveal and disclose himself to his people, we learned that the Godhead is a community, a divine family: one substance in three Persons.

Pope St. John Paul II teaches us this truth:

> It has been said, in a beautiful and profound way, that our God in his deepest mystery is not a solitude, but a family, since he has in himself fatherhood, sonship and the essence of the family, which is love (Address at Puebla de Los Angeles, Mexico, 1979).

Saint Paul, the rabbi-turned-apostle and student of the esteemed elder Gamaliel, saw no conflict with the oneness of God and the revelation of the Holy Trinity. He defended the unicity of God at every turn and with every step of his apostolic mission. While in Athens, the revered city-state of the false god Athena and the home of Greek philosophy, the apostle could have compromised and attempted to explain the Triune God with tri-theistic language, but he did not. He would not allow any possible adulteration of the oneness of God. He did not fall into any blend of paganism or give any leeway to the pantheon of old. Instead, he used the multiplicity of the false gods as a way of denouncing idolatry and pointing the Athenians to the one, true God.

Boldly preaching at the Areopagus, Paul told the Greeks:

Athenians, I see how extremely religious you are
in every way. For as I went through the city and
looked carefully at the objects of your worship,
I found among them an altar with the inscrip-
tion, "To an unknown god." What therefore
you worship as unknown, this I proclaim to you.
The God who made the world and everything
in it, he who is Lord of heaven and earth, does
not live in shrines made by human hands, nor is
he served by human hands, as though he needed
anything, since he himself gives to all mortals
life and breath and all things. From one ancestor
he made all nations to inhabit the whole earth,
and he allotted the times of their existence and
the boundaries of the places where they would
live, so that they would search for God and perhaps grope for him and find him—though indeed he is not far from each one of us. For "In
him we live and move and have our being"; as
even some of your own poets have said, "For we
too are his offspring."

Since we are God's offspring, we ought not
to think that the deity is like gold, or silver, or
stone, an image formed by the art and imagination of mortals. While God has overlooked the
times of human ignorance, now he commands
all people everywhere to repent, because he has
fixed a day on which he will have the world
judged in righteousness by a man whom he has
appointed, and of this he has given assurance to
all by raising him from the dead (Acts 17:22–31).

The early Christians were unshakably monotheistic
and rejoiced in the oneness of God. They also saw the

unveiling of the Holy Trinity as a gift and a further disclosure of love by God. By knowing him more intimately, they could love him more selflessly. Knowing that the Messiah was God himself, and that he had come to us, was a mystery that elevated their joy and gave immense zeal to their way of life. Such consolation was palpable in the writings of St. Paul:

> Hence, as to the eating of food offered to idols, we know that "no idol in the world really exists," and that "there is no God but one." Indeed, even though there may be so-called gods in heaven or on earth—as in fact there are many gods and many lords—yet for us there is one God, the Father, from whom are all things and for whom we exist, and one Lord, Jesus Christ, through whom are all things and through whom we exist (1 Cor. 8:4–6).

God is true not because we think it, feel it, prefer it, desire it, or need it. God is objectively, distinctively true. He is, as the *Catechism of the Catholic Church* teaches, "infinitely perfect and blessed in himself" (1). This was the bedrock of the early Church's faith. It is the bedrock of a healthy and strong faith today.

As Christians, have we fallen into a lackadaisical approach toward God? Have we compromised or adjusted the revelations of God to accommodate our culture and its behavior? Do we boldly speak and share the powerful truth that there is one God, all-powerful and ever-living, who has been revealed to us as a Divine Family and desires us to be a part of it?

A Cosmos of Petty Gods

As enlightened as we think we are in the twenty-first century West, we must speak of what is observable: That as a civilization we have backslid into more-developed versions of former paganism and barbarity. Our technological and scientific successes have created a façade of development, an illusion of advancement. We think we are so progressive and advanced, when in fact we are actually regressing as a human civilization. We have constructed a house of cards but have convinced ourselves (and forced the rest of the world to believe) that our foundation is steady and our current trajectory noble and beneficial to humanity.

We are at such a level of delusion and confusion that the singularity of God and his Son, Jesus Christ, is overshadowed by a subjective collection of personal deities. Regressing back to the times of pagan myths, we have placed Jesus Christ into a peculiar pantheon of false gods of our own devising. The Lord Jesus is trivialized and made to be one more personal god.

When humanity abandons God's own revelation of himself, then anything is justified. Anything can become a god. And even Jesus Christ can be turned into anything a person wants. This also means that the Lord Jesus cannot be fully known, loved, or followed. For when the God who is Love has been deformed and turned into something other than what he truly is, then love itself becomes deformed. When the Creator is abandoned, the creature diminishes. As Love is abandoned, our ability to love shrinks. Only in the full truth of the living God, and through his Son, Jesus Christ, can we fully know love.

Pope St. John Paul II taught in his encyclical, *Redemptor Hominis:*

Man cannot live without love. He remains a being that is incomprehensible for himself, his life is
senseless, if love is not revealed to him, if he does
not encounter love, if he does not experience it
and make it his own, if he does not participate
intimately in it. This, as has already been said,
is why Christ the Redeemer "fully reveals man
to himself." If we may use the expression, this
is the human dimension of the mystery of the
Redemption. In this dimension man finds again
the greatness, dignity, and value that belong to
his humanity. In the mystery of the Redemption
man becomes newly "expressed" and, in a way,
is newly created. He is newly created! (10).

If the true God is abandoned for personal deities an-
imated by the world's fads, not only are we unable to
know what love is, we also cannot truly know *ourselves*.
Full self-knowledge, too, is only possible through the
mystery of Jesus Christ. John Paul II continues:

The man who wishes to understand himself thor-
oughly—and not just in accordance with immediate, partial, often superficial, and even illusory
standards and measures of his being—he must
with his unrest, uncertainty, and even his weakness and sinfulness, with his life and death, draw
near to Christ. He must, so to speak, enter into
him with all his own self, he must "appropriate"
and assimilate the whole of the reality of the In-
carnation and Redemption in order to find himself. If this profound process takes place within
him, he then bears fruit not only of adoration
of God but also of deep wonder at himself (10).

Jesus Loves You

On one occasion early in my priesthood, I was venting to a mentor about the lack of knowledge or gratitude many people show toward the sacrificial love of Jesus Christ. It was discouraging for me to see so much indifference to the loving kindness the Lord Jesus has for us, and I was giving voice to this frustration.

This particular mentor was a senior priest who in his decades of priestly ministry had seen pretty much everything. As I moved from point to point, he gently and kindly nodded his head. After a while, I finished my diatribe, and he gave me a good stare. Then he said to me, "We tell people, 'Jesus loves you' and we think they understand. We get frustrated when they don't respond to the love of Jesus Christ, which we think is so clear."

He cleared his throat and continued with a stronger pitch, "But we take so much for granted today. We say 'Jesus loves you,' but people don't understand Jesus, love, or even themselves. We have to start with the basics, with an initial proclamation of Jesus, of love, and of ourselves before God. We have to learn from the early Church and proclaim the gospel anew to a generation of unbelievers. Only after we give this core teaching to those around us can we truly say that people have dismissed the invitation Jesus Christ offers to us of his saving love. Otherwise, people are only rejecting what they do not understand."

We all have to learn these truths. I've had to learn (and re-learn) them as a disciple and as a priest. The truths of God are so different from the lies of our fallen world that we need the constant help of grace and the witness of others to know God, love him and others, and even to love ourselves. We either choose this path, or another path will be thrust upon us.

And so, as a neo-secular form of paganism takes over the Western heart, all the world's preoccupations—pleasure, power, comfort, autonomy, human affection, the market, political parties and ideologies—come to form a broken pantheon in the cosmos of fallen humanity, devoid of grace and marked by a raw restlessness that cannot be filled and only compels ever-greater expressions of self-worship and a will to power.

The early Church announced the oneness of God alongside the coming of the Messiah, the long-awaited anointed Savior. This announcement lent itself to the proclamation:

> Beloved, let us love one another, because love is from God; everyone who loves is born of God and knows God. Whoever does not love does not know God, for God is love. God's love was revealed among us in this way: God sent his only Son into the world so that we might live through him. In this is love, not that we loved God but that he loved us and sent his Son to be the atoning sacrifice for our sins. Beloved, since God loved us so much, we also ought to love one another. No one has ever seen God; if we love one another, God lives in us, and his love is perfected in us (1 John 4:7–12).

The gospel inspired the early Church to present the one God as merciful and kind, slow to anger and abounding in goodness. They showed that he was neither cruel, nor barbarous, nor petty. They showed the way of God to be a way guided by reason and love, part of a binding covenant that makes us the children of God. The early Christians' faith, way of life, and message modeled for the fallen world the tenderness, affection, and loving affection of God.

As believers, we need to examine our own hearts. Have we fallen prey to the tendency to create our own gods, or to change the one true God so that he is merely a reflection of ourselves or our own beliefs and desires? Do we understand the radical singularity of Jesus Christ and abandon all notions that run contrary to his teachings and revelations? When we speak of God's oneness, do we also speak of his love and kindness for all?

Renewed and Degraded Paganism

Although the sovereign selves of the twenty-first-century West are quick to distinguish themselves from the naivete and lack of sophistication of the paganism of old, as a civilization we are reverting back to their beliefs and way of life. The allure of paganism and its idolatry is always whispering outside the human heart, and many are eager to open their hearts to its influence.

It would surprise the contemporary person, who prides himself on his enlightenment, to realize how similar his worldview is to the pagans'. Modern man's self-created pantheon—worshipping the self and human wisdom—is not far different from the ancient pantheon of false gods and goddesses.

In making such a comparison, however, we don't want to insult the transcendental and sometimes sincere views of the ancient pagans. Many of them at least held to something beyond themselves; they humbly accepted the traditions of their forebears; and they sought to worship and engage with their deities. Though contemporary relativists and syncretists are like the ancient pagans in some respects, they are woefully below them when it comes to deference to one's tribe, the desire for worship, and the quest for an encounter with divinity.

The post-modern person has abandoned all semblance of tradition. He believes that he must create his own truth, mold his own myths, and bow before his own pantheon of pseudo-gods. The pagans of old would have considered the contemporary person as a freak and an ungrateful dissident.

As Christians today, do we sometimes live as if we were in a cosmos of petty gods? Do we fill our minds and hearts with human whims instead of God's truth? Have we created our own deities that we worship on our terms and according to our preferences?

The Barbarism of Paganism

When we have a return to paganism, we undoubtedly have a return to barbarity.

In ancient times, outside of God's people in Israel, the world was viewed as a bleak place. There was no certainty or constancy in creation. The Greek gods were just projections of the most debauched Greeks: vengeful, capricious, and petty; jealous, vain, and lacking in justice or mercy.

In such a world, fear triumphed and barbarity was the rule of the day. Or to put it another way: as the gods went, fallen humanity followed.

The pagan myths, accordingly, presented a world without love, hope, or mercy. There was no reason, no interior moral logic to the world, and no cause for goodness and peace. The world was weighed down by horror and distress. Humanity's fate was consumed by panic and fright. Life was seen as nothing more than a nightmare of angst and dread.

This is the spirit of the world to which Western civilization is reverting. It is the dark spirit that animates the abortion movement, the extremes of LGBTQ+ activism, the war on marriage and family, the propagation of pornography, human trafficking, and the objectification of others, and the growing acceptance of euthanasia and assisted suicide. It is the backdrop of the twentieth century's wars of irreligion (which were far more severe than any war of religion) and of the fallen thinking behind communism, fascism, and human exploitation by the wealthy. It is the Luciferic godfather of meaninglessness, nihilism, and self-destruction, reviving paganism's barbarism and misery.

In contrast to the brutality of the pagan way of life, the early Christians saw in the life and ministry of Jesus Christ a different way. Receiving the promise of salvation through the Paschal Mystery of the Lord Jesus—from his passion, death, and resurrection—the early Christians sought to follow his way of sacrificial love, compassion, and selfless service. By this way, they would work out their salvation and seek to offer the saving graces of God to all men and women.

Following the example of the Lord Jesus, and the first Christian martyr St. Stephen, the early Christians prayed for those who persecuted them, welcomed anyone who desired salvation in Christ, served everyone—even those outside of their circle, which was unheard of in the ancient world—and accepted sufferings and rejection for the sake of truth, goodness, and beauty. Into a fallen world of paganism, the Church announced the fullness of one God. In a fallen world of cruelty, the Church proclaimed the love of Jesus Christ. In a fallen world of vengeance, the Church announced divine mercy. In a fallen world of tribalism and strife, the Church lived a universal brotherhood of compassion and service.

As followers of Jesus Christ, do we continue his work of salvation through loving sacrifice and service? Do we let ourselves fall into the barbarism of the unbeliever? Do we show our faith by our good deeds?

One God, One Mediator

Into such a confused and violent world, the Dawn from on high has broken upon us (Luke 1:78). God's chosen people Israel was prepared to recognize and receive the Messiah, and in the fullness of time, that anointed Savior came to us! (Gal. 4:4–7). In an utterly gratuitous and surprising twist, the anticipated Messiah was God himself!

No one could have anticipated such a fulfillment. In all the longings of his Hebrew heart, not even the prophet Isaiah—who was the closest to prophesying about the anointed Savior—could have imagined that God himself would be the fulfillment of the messianic promises. The living and true God became a man and "pitched his tent" with us (John 1:14). As St. John observed:

> And I heard a loud voice from the throne saying, "See, the home of God is among mortals. He will dwell with them; they will be his peoples, and God himself will be with them" (Rev. 21:3).

The proclamation of the one true God, who is Wisdom and Love, shook the pagan worldview and its sanctioned maliciousness to its very core. Such a claim among

God's people, however, might have been dismissed by unbelievers as mere nonsense, delusional thinking, or wishful meanderings, until that reality became tangibly present in Jesus Christ, God made man. In him, the one God was flesh, walking among us, and declaring to us his love and mercy.

The Lord Jesus gives the solemn invitation:

> Do not let your hearts be troubled. Believe in God, believe also in me. In my Father's house there are many dwelling places. If it were not so, would I have told you that I go to prepare a place for you? And if I go and prepare a place for you, I will come again and will take you to myself, so that where I am, there you may be also. And you know the way to the place where I am going." Thomas said to him, "Lord, we do not know where you are going. How can we know the way?" Jesus said to him, "I am the way, and the truth, and the life. No one comes to the Father except through me. If you know me, you will know my Father also. From now on you do know him and have seen him" (John 14:1–7).

In his apostolic preaching, St. Peter shows the unity of the Father and the Son by the Holy Spirit, and how the Lord Jesus, Son of God and son of David, has been given to us:

> This Jesus God raised up, and of that all of us are witnesses. Being therefore exalted at the right hand of God, and having received from the Father the promise of the Holy Spirit, he has

poured out this that you both see and hear. For David did not ascend into the heavens, but he himself says, "The Lord said to my Lord, 'Sit at my right hand, until I make your enemies your footstool.'"

Therefore, let the entire house of Israel know with certainty that God has made him both Lord and Messiah, this Jesus whom you crucified (Acts 2:32–36).

Paul echoes this teaching, showing us the oneness of the Father and the Son and pointing us to the Lord Jesus as the means of coming to know the Father:

This is right and is acceptable in the sight of God our Savior, who desires everyone to be saved and to come to the knowledge of the truth. For there is one God; there is also one mediator between God and humankind, Christ Jesus, himself human, who gave himself a ransom for all—this was attested at the right time (1 Tim 2:3–6).

These profound declarations were the core of the proclaimed message of the early Church. In a world ruled by false gods, the Church—fulfilling the vocation first given to Israel and going supremely beyond it—announced the kingdom of the one true God, living as a divine family, and the one mediator sent to ransom us from sin so that we can be welcomed into the house of our Father. As the early Church carried this gospel mantle, so we are called joyfully to carry it today, reminding a world wrapped in paganism of the one God and one mediator and the immense love that is offered to humanity.

Do we speak openly and without shame of the one true God and one Mediator between God and man? Do we fight against the neo-paganism of our day? Do we defend the majesty and holiness of God in our culture and society today?

God With Us

The Son of God did not come as a removed figure falling from the skies. He was not spit out of the mind of his divine Father or conceived from a peculiar sexual encounter, as was commonly said of divinities in the myths of Greece and Rome. When he came, it was not as a ghost or a theophany that merely appeared to be human. The Second Person of the Holy Trinity was born of woman as a true man.

As St. Paul taught,

> But when the time had fully come, God sent forth his Son, born of woman, born under the law, to redeem those who were under the law, so that we might receive adoption as sons (Gal. 4:4–5).

The divine Son became a fully human being and experienced all things that are truly human:

> Since, then, we have a great high priest who has passed through the heavens, Jesus, the Son of God, let us hold fast to our confession. For we do not have a high priest who is unable to sympathize with our weaknesses, but we have one who in every respect has been tested as we are, yet without sin. Let us therefore approach the

throne of grace with boldness, so that we may
receive mercy and find grace to help in time of
need (Heb. 4:14–16).

The Lord Jesus showed us our dignity and worth as the
children of God and taught us how to live and so work
out our salvation in him:

> The true light that enlightens every man was
> coming into the world. He was in the world, and
> the world was made through him, yet the world
> knew him not. He came to his own home, and
> his own people received him not. But to all who
> received him, who believed in his name, he gave
> power to become children of God; who were
> born, not of blood nor of the will of the flesh nor
> of the will of man, but of God (John 1:9–13).

The Second Vatican Council teaches us:

> For, by his incarnation, he, the Son of God, has
> in a certain way united himself with each man.
> He worked with human hands, He thought with
> a human mind. He acted with a human will and
> with a human heart he loved (*Gaudium et Spes*
> 22).

The Second Person of the Holy Trinity took on human flesh in Jesus of Nazareth. He came as the fullness
of all God's revelation. All that humanity had discerned
of God through the light of natural reason, and all that
was supernaturally revealed to humanity about God, was
recapitulated and fulfilled in Jesus Christ. As the Second

Vatican Council teaches us, "By this revelation then, the deepest truth about God and the salvation of man shines out for our sake in Christ, who is both the mediator and the fullness of all revelation" (*Dei Verbum* 2).

At Caesarea-Philippi, St. Peter announced that this God-Man was the long-awaited Savior: "You are the Messiah, the Son of the living God" (Matt. 16:16). As did Martha at Bethany: "Yes, Lord, I believe that you are the Messiah, the Son of God, the one coming into the world" (John 11:27).

Although fully human, and coming as the Savior of humanity, the Second Person of the Trinity did not lose his divinity. Jesus Christ was truly God and truly man. As such, he was the model of what it means to be human. In his life and work, the Lord Jesus showed humanity how we are to live and serve others. The Second Vatican Council taught:

> In reality it is only in the mystery of the Word made flesh that the mystery of man truly becomes clear. For Adam, the first man, was a type of him who was to come, Christ the Lord, Christ the new Adam, in the very revelation of the mystery of the Father and of his love, fully reveals man to himself and brings to light his most high calling (*Gaudium et Spes* 22).

By understanding the human identity of Jesus Christ, humanity can see a brighter reflection of itself and can better and more deeply hear and appreciate the Lord's teachings and witness among us. The Lord Jesus came to us, taught us, and lived among us. He does not teach as an outsider but as someone within the human family.

One Lord, One Faith, One Baptism

Bringing together the divine truths of the oneness of God, the triune nature of the Godhead, and the one mediator sent to us as Messiah and Lord, the early Church lived the life given to it by the Lord Jesus. The community of believers fiercely lived the way they witnessed the Lord himself live. They labored and suffered to live as he lived, to love as he loved, and to serve as he served. In living the way of the Lord, they reflected the unity and the love of God.

Walking the way of the Lord together, "They devoted themselves to the apostles' teaching and fellowship, to the breaking of bread and the prayers" (Acts 2:42).

Accordingly, Paul stressed the unity of the believers:

> There is one body and one Spirit, just as you were called to the one hope of your calling, one Lord, one faith, one baptism, one God and Father of all, who is above all and through all and in all (Eph. 4:4–6).

In this way of life, they reflected what they believed. The behavior of the early Church didn't determine its beliefs. The beliefs given to it by the Lord Jesus determined its way of life. In contrast to the relativism and sentimentalism of today, the early believers of the Lord Jesus clung to the revelations—the words and deeds—he gave them. These sacred teachings became the foundation, sustenance, and impetus to the entire life of the early Church. The Church believed, lived, and proclaimed—in the midst of a world possessed by paganism—the truth of one God and one mediator.

As we seek to be disciples of the Lord Jesus in our age, we are called to the same conviction, fidelity, and boldness. In the face of the neo-paganism and self-worship of our day, we are called daily to announce the truth of one God and one mediator.

In our lives as Christians, do we reflect the unity and love of God? Does our parish life show what we believe? Do we live what we believe? Or do we change our beliefs according to how we want to live? Are we bold in our declaration of one God and one Mediator?

Application to Our Lives

Declarations of Discipleship

- I believe and worship the one true God, Father, Son, and Holy Spirit.

- I will not fall into the pantheons of false gods.

- I will speak and defend the majesty of the one God, living and true.

Examination of Conscience

The following questions are given as an examination of conscience on our fidelity to the one, true God:

- Do I wholeheartedly believe in the one true God?

- Have I created my own pantheon of false gods?

- Have I ordered my entire life to the one true God?

- Are there other gods in my life that I am willing to give more time and attention to rather than the one true God?

- Am I obedient to the covenant and law of God?

- Am I ashamed to let others know of my faith?

- Do I speak about the one God and one mediator without shame or embarrassment?

- Do I place God's will ahead of my own?

- Do I live my life mindful of God in all that I say and do?

- Do I actively participate in the life of my parish?

Having made this examination of conscience, I recommend that you go and make a good confession based on these points.

Key Points

Here are some points to bear in mind as a help in speaking to our fellow believers and to unbelievers around us about the truth of God:

1. There is one God, living and true.

2. The living God is not the *highest* of gods, or the most *powerful* of gods. There are *no* other gods.

3. God exists whether we know it, feel it, or prefer it. The existence and majesty of God is

beyond our intellect, feelings, and preferences. He is real, infinitely perfect and blessed in himself.

4. The mystery of the Holy Trinity expands our understanding of the one true God.

5. The Trinity is not "three gods." There is only one God, who exists as a kind of divine family, Father, Son, and Holy Spirit.

6. There is only one mediator between God and humanity. The long-awaited Messiah was God himself. God the Son, the Second Person of the Holy Trinity, took on our human nature and by his life, death, and resurrection brought redemption to our fallen state.

7. Jesus Christ is true God and true man. He shows us the face of our Father and reveals the tenderness and loving kindness of God to us.

8. There is a contemporary resurgence of paganism as many people form their own gods and are engaging in self-worship and so rebelling against the one true God.

9. Believers must avoid the allure of the pantheon of false gods and remain steadfast in their knowledge and worship of the one true God.

10. The lives of believers and of Christian communities are to show the love and mercy of God.

Devotional Exercise

The *Shema*

> Hear, O Israel,
> The Lord is our God, the Lord alone.
> You shall love the Lord your God with all your
>   heart,
> and with all your soul, and with all your
>   might. Keep these words
> that I am commanding you today in your heart.

> —DEUTERONOMY 6:4–6

Act of Faith

> O my God, I firmly believe
> that you are one God in three divine Persons,
>   Father, Son, and Holy Spirit.
> I believe that your divine Son became man and
>   died for our sins and that he will come
> to judge the living and the dead.
> I believe these and all the truths
> which the Holy Catholic Church teaches be-
>   cause you have revealed them
> who are eternal truth and wisdom,
> who can neither deceive nor be deceived.
>   In this faith I intend to live and die.
> Amen.

Suscipe (St. Ignatius of Loyola)

> Take, Lord, and receive all my liberty,
> my memory, my understanding,
> and my entire will,
> All I have and call my own.
> You have given all to me.
> To you, Lord, I return it.

Everything is yours; do with it what you will.
Give me only your love and your grace,
that is enough for me.
Amen.

Stations of the Cross

As you pray the stations of the cross, ask for the grace to avoid the false worship of our day. Stay focused on the one true God. Grieve and mourn for our world as it deludes itself with paganism and self-worship: "Daughters of Jerusalem, do not weep for me, but weep for yourselves and for your children. For behold, the days are coming when they will say, 'Blessed are the barren, and the wombs that never bore, and the breasts that never gave suck!' Then they will begin to say to the mountains, 'Fall on us'; and to the hills, 'Cover us.' For if they do this when the wood is green, what will happen when it is dry?" (Luke 23:28–31).

Rosary Suggestions

The next time you pray the rosary, consider these points:

Joyful Mysteries: The faith and reverence of the Blessed Virgin Mary and St. Joseph for the majesty and will of God.

Luminous Mysteries: The loving devotion the Lord Jesus had for the Father and his faithfulness and obedience to his will.

Sorrowful Mysteries: The willingness to suffer for the love of God and humanity. The unjust persecution, tribulations, and torture that Jesus endured in trust and obedience to God.

Glorious Mysteries: The great joy that awaits those who love God. The eternal happiness that has been won by the Paschal Mystery of the Lord Jesus and his offer of eternal life to those who trust and are devoted to him.

CHAPTER TWO

THE GOSPEL, NOT CLEVERLY DEVISED MYTHS

How sweet are your words to my taste,
sweeter than honey to my mouth!
Through your precepts I get understanding;
therefore I hate every false way.
Your word is a lamp to my feet
and a light to my path.

—PSALM 119:103–105

The sacred scriptures are the living word of God. When the People of God engage the word of God, powerful things happen, and errors and misunderstandings are corrected.

On one occasion, as I was speaking to a small group of people during a break at a conference, I stressed the

importance of the Bible and how essential it is for believers to have a substantial knowledge of Scripture. In
response, a woman—I will call her Judy—perked up and
said, "Well, sure, the Bible is good. But I don't like the
Old Testament God."

It took a lot for me not to do a backflip at such a comment, but I smiled and resolved to help Judy to understand why such a perspective is misplaced. It has been my
experience that people who make such comments usually
have not actually read the Old Testament (and perhaps
not most of the New Testament, either). They assert such
things with an awkward boldness but usually not much
knowledge. I knew that a conversation was needed and
so I began.

"It's wonderful that you see the goodness of the Bible
and understand the importance of reading and knowing
Sacred Scripture. Regarding your comment about the
'Old Testament God,' I just want to clarify some things."

Honestly, at this point Judy looked completely disin-
terested! But there were other people listening and so I
continued.

"You know, there is only one God. There isn't an "Old
Testament God" and a "New Testament God." There is
only one God, and he has given us one plan of salvation.
The singular plan that he has given to us is contained
in both the Old and New Testaments. The two testaments have a dynamic relationship. The Old Testament
prepared us for the coming of the Messiah, our anointed
Savior, and the New Testament shows us his arrival and
his work of redemption among us."

There still wasn't an active response, but now Judy was
making eye contact and seemed to have *some* level of en-
gagement, and so I continued.

"The interaction between the Old Testament and New

Testament is the most exciting drama in human history. Our forefathers in the Faith taught us that 'the new is hidden in the old, and the old is revealed in the new.' Our efforts to see the work of God in the Old Testament help us understand what God accomplished in the New Testament. It's not two gods battling it out, but one God and one plan of salvation contained in a single sacred narrative. In these two testaments are shifts and perspectives, a sacred cause and effort, a powerful sequence of events that give redemptive meaning and purpose to the stories of our own lives."

Now Judy seemed confused, but not embarrassed. Eventually, she responded, "Maybe. I just don't like the Old Testament God . . . or whatever he's called. He's always mean and angry. I like Jesus. He's happy and he makes me feel good about myself."

Those words spoke volumes of misunderstanding; but Judy was sincere. And so, I asked, "What particular accounts or events are you referencing? What scenes from the Old Testament make you uncomfortable with God?"

I was anticipating one of the usual responses: the temptation of Abraham, the binding of Isaac, Sodom and Gomorrah, or some other troubling passage. To my shock, though, Judy could not cite a single specific account that troubled her. She just "knew" there was an Old Testament God who was angry and mean-spirited and that the New Testament contained the nice, loving God.

After the last exchange, I realized that, despite her presence at the conference, Judy was a neophyte to the Christian faith. Although sacramentalized and having been raised in a Christian home, she lacked encounter with the Bible and fundamental Christian teaching. Judy was just one more regrettable casualty of our society-wide biblical and doctrinal illiteracy—a baby Christian in an adult body. This realization changed my approach.

"It's okay," I said. "It can be hard to cite examples from the Bible. But as you share your thoughts on your perspective of God, I want to emphasize how essential the Bible is to us as believers. In the Bible, we have the account of God's action among us. It tells the story of God's words and deeds in the world. We must read and study it if we want to understand who God truly is. That way, we won't fall into turning God into something he isn't, nor unknowingly accept the contemporary myths and cultural lies and misrepresentations about him. You see?"

It was clear that I had extended the conversation beyond Judy's interest level and that of others around us. I let my last comments be the conclusion. I smiled, made a joke about the weather, and then looked to move on. It's my hope that the points made to Judy might bear fruit and lead to a true reading and studying of the Bible.

Have we misunderstood the purpose of the Old Testament and tried to separate it from the New Testament? Do we have a warped, one-sided view of God and his revelations? Do we welcome the one, true God into our hearts and seek to follow the one plan of salvation in our lives?

The Revelations of God

It is a humbling and powerful reality that God, the All-Powerful and Ancient of Days, has chosen to speak and act in our midst. It should be a spiritual thunderbolt to realize that God has come to us, disclosed to us knowledge of his very self. As should the further realization that he has done this because he *loves* us, seeks fellowship with us, and wants us (undeservingly) to be adopted members of his own family unto eternity.

In the life and public ministry of the Lord Jesus, divine revelation as contained in oral tradition and in the Hebrew scriptures—which he knew, quoted, taught, and expected his disciples to know—were the source and impetus of his saving work.

The early Church that Jesus founded likewise clung to Scripture as a bulwark against the pagan influences around them. In his five sermons contained in the Acts of the Apostles, St. Peter referenced, cited, and relied upon the scriptures to show that Jesus of Nazareth was the long-awaited Messiah, was true God and true man, and that his passion, death, and resurrection are the source of eternal life for those who love him (Acts 2:14–39; Acts 3:11–4:4; Acts 4:8–12; Acts 5:29–32; Acts 10:34–43).

In their own ways, all the sermons are summations of Old Testament prophecies, promises, typological persons, events, and institutions, and declarations of their fulfillment in Jesus Christ. Rich in biblical meaning and interpretation, they show how the scriptures are essential if we are going to understand and accept who God is and who Jesus Christ is among us.

For example, in his sermon at Pentecost, Peter preached,

> Fellow Israelites, I may say to you confidently of our ancestor David that he both died and was buried, and his tomb is with us to this day. Since he was a prophet, he knew that God had sworn with an oath to him that he would put one of his descendants on his throne. Foreseeing this, David spoke of the resurrection of the Messiah, saying, "He was not abandoned to Hades, nor did his flesh experience corruption."

This Jesus God raised up, and of that all of us are witnesses. Being therefore exalted at the right hand of God, and having received from the Father the promise of the Holy Spirit, he has poured out this that you both see and hear. For David did not ascend into the heavens, but he himself says, "The Lord said to my Lord, 'Sit at my right hand, until I make your enemies your footstool.'"

Therefore let the entire house of Israel know with certainty that God has made him both Lord and Messiah, this Jesus whom you crucified (Acts 2:29–36).

Within the apostolic community, St. Stephen followed a similar pattern. One of our first deacons and the protomartyr of the Church, Stephen announced and witnessed to the lordship of Jesus Christ. As he was about to stoned, he preached a sermon steeped in the narrative of salvation history. At its conclusion, the holy deacon proclaimed,

You stiff-necked people, uncircumcised in heart and ears, you are forever opposing the Holy Spirit, just as your ancestors used to do. Which of the prophets did your ancestors not persecute? They killed those who foretold the coming of the Righteous One, and now you have become his betrayers and murderers. You are the ones that received the law as ordained by angels, and yet you have not kept it (Acts 7:51–53).

The sacred scriptures had been the guide and the course all along the way. Dismissing the myths of paganism and casting out bad spirits, the early Christians held to the revealed truths of God. No cost, even martyrdom, could sway the followers of the Lord Jesus to abandon that path.

St. Paul put it bluntly, teaching us:

> For whatever was written in former days was written for our instruction, so that by steadfastness and by the encouragement of the scriptures we might have hope (Rom. 15:4).

Later he stressed this point to St. Timothy (and to all Christians):

> But as for you, continue in what you have learned and firmly believed, knowing from whom you learned it, and how from childhood you have known the sacred writings that are able to instruct you for salvation through faith in Christ Jesus. All scripture is inspired by God and is useful for teaching, for reproof, for correction, and for training in righteousness, so that everyone who belongs to God may be proficient, equipped for every good work (2 Tim. 3:14–17).

The early Church did not see a contradiction between the Old Testament and the New, therefore, but cherished the former and welcomed the revelation of the latter as the heart of their faith, life, and work. Receiving the oral and written revelations of God in all their entirety, they knew that there was no reliable knowledge of salvation—and so no Christian discipleship—without learning and living by the revelations of God.

As Christians, do we realize the importance of God's revelations in our discipleship? Do we make time to read and study the Bible and conform our lives to its truths? Do we fall into the modern-day myths and cultural distortions and misrepresentations of God?

The "Gospel"

Some years ago, I was called to a local hospital to pray with someone and give him the consolation of the sacraments. As I approached the hospital, a large woman, seeing my Roman collar, stopped me at the door and bluntly asked, "Are you a true Bible-believing minister?" Being acquainted with Protestant religious terminology, I smiled, nodded my head in the affirmative, and boldly responded, "Yes, ma'am, I'm full-gospel!"

The woman was relieved and said to me, "We need more ministers like you." She then gave me some prayer intentions relating to her family members.

In this exchange, the woman and I shared some language but I suspect we meant different things. For myself, "full gospel" is more holistic than adherence to the teachings of the Bible (or a certain group's interpretations of them). It includes the entirety of God's revelation, communicated in both written and oral form and preserved by the Church.

The sum total of all God's revelations to us are fulfilled in the life and teachings of Jesus Christ. The Father has spoken through his Son by the power of the Holy Spirit. The Son, the Incarnate Word, sums up all that God has ever spoken and done among humanity. As St. John teaches us,

> In the beginning was the Word, and the Word was with God, and the Word was God. He was in the beginning with God. All things came into

being through him, and without him not one
thing came into being. What has come into being in him was life, and the life was the light of
all people (John 1:1–4).

St. Paul echoes this teaching when he writes,

For in him [Christ] every one of God's promises
is a "Yes." For this reason it is through him that
we say the "Amen," to the glory of God (2 Cor.
1:20).

The narrative of Jesus' life and teachings is commonly
called *the gospel*—the good news. The four particular, inspired, canonical written accounts of his life are called
Gospels. In a broader sense, however, we might use the
word *gospel* to apply to the collation of all God's revelations in word and deed, as they are fully contained,
unveiled, and fulfilled in Jesus Christ. This gospel in all
its fullness is the definitive, inerrant, and trustworthy
self-narrative of God to the human family.

The Second Vatican Council beautifully explains:

In his goodness and wisdom God chose to reveal
himself and to make known to us the hidden purpose of his will (see Eph. 1:9) by which through
Christ, the Word made flesh, man might in the
Holy Spirit have access to the Father and come
to share in the divine nature (see Eph. 2:18; 2
Pet. 1:4). Through this revelation, therefore, the
invisible God (see Col. 1;15, 1 Tim. 1:17) out
of the abundance of his love speaks to men as
friends (see Exod. 33:11; John 15:14–15) and lives

among them (see Bar. 3:38), so that he may invite and take them into fellowship with himself. This plan of revelation is realized by deeds and words having an inner unity: the deeds wrought by God in the history of salvation manifest and confirm the teaching and realities signified by the words, while the words proclaim the deeds and clarify the mystery contained in them.

The council's teaching on divine revelation goes on to add that Jesus

completes the work of salvation which his Father gave him to do (see John 5:36; John 17:4). To see Jesus is to see his Father (John 14:9). For this reason Jesus perfected revelation by fulfilling it through his whole work of making himself present and manifesting himself: through his words and deeds, his signs and wonders, but especially through his death and glorious resurrection from the dead and final sending of the Spirit of truth. Moreover he confirmed with divine testimony what revelation proclaimed, that God is with us to free us from the darkness of sin and death, and to raise us up to life eternal (*Dei Verbum 2*).

The holistic gospel, then, is not reducible to a book and not, as cynical critics imagine, a collection of clever myths, but the fullness of God's intimate sharing of himself. In contrast to the pagan myths of old and the neo-pagan myths of today, this gospel stands firm and can never be compromised.

Do I avoid the exaggerations of unbelievers in their approach to God? Do I allow the gospel to teach and correct me about God and his true identity? Do I seek to prevent my heart from forming its own personal gospel?

Historical Reality Versus Mythical Fantasies

Unlike myths, the gospel is based on historical facts. It is not "Jesus and the Seven Dwarves." Its events are attested, chronicled, archived, preserved. They are not fiction, and neither are they a parable that uses fiction to convey moral lessons or wishful thinking. The gospel is not real because it's intellectually satisfying or because it provides emotional consolation. It is not real because it's a cherished family tradition. It is not real because it describes a way of love and mercy.

The gospel is not real because of anything we value in it or just because we *want* it to be.

Apart from any movements of our hearts, hands, or minds, the gospel stands on its own. It is really real. Its events truly occurred in our world.

The early Church understood this powerful reality. They staked everything on it. The early followers of the Lord Jesus had no time for myths, exaggerations, or mere comforting thoughts. They were focused on the Lord Jesus and his real mysteries.

> We declare to you what was from the beginning, what we have heard, what we have seen with our eyes, what we have looked at and touched with our hands, concerning the word of life—this life was revealed, and we have seen it and testify to

it, and declare to you the eternal life that was with the Father and was revealed to us—we declare to you what we have seen and heard so that you also may have fellowship with us; and truly our fellowship is with the Father and with his Son Jesus Christ (1 John 1–3).

That body of believers took to heart Paul's admonition:

In the presence of God and of Christ Jesus, who is to judge the living and the dead, and in view of his appearing and his kingdom, I solemnly urge you: proclaim the message; be persistent whether the time is favorable or unfavorable; convince, rebuke, and encourage, with the utmost patience in teaching. For the time is coming when people will not put up with sound doctrine, but having itching ears, they will accumulate for themselves teachers to suit their own desires, and will turn away from listening to the truth and wander away to myths. As for you, always be sober, endure suffering, do the work of an evangelist, carry out your ministry fully (2 Tim. 4:1–5).

The early Church was thus consumed with a drive to share this real gospel with all humanity. The early disciples called out error, denounced mythical interpretations of the gospel, repudiated false teachers, abjured fables and fallacies presenting themselves as gospel; and they did this doctrinally charitable work with unquestioned sternness and boldness. Without apology, the early disciples rejected any effort to adulterate the truth of the gospel. They held—and persevered in—an absolute surety and confidence in its realness.

Have I ever fallen into the temptation to think that the gospel is just a bunch of fairy tales? Do I realize the historical and real nature of all that God has done among us? Do I allow the historical reality of the gospel to convict me in my discipleship and compel me to prepare for judgment and eternity?

It Happened Right Here

Many years ago, as a graduate student, I spent a summer with a Christian Palestinian family in Bethlehem. It was my first visit to the Holy Land, and, as it does for many new pilgrims, it rocked my world.

One thing struck me immediately. Throughout the Holy Land, you can see the word *hic* inscribed in various locations, like churches and alleyways. This simple word, Latin for "here," was written as a reminder to the believer that the events recorded in the Gospels all happened in those places.

They were true, historical events. They occurred on the site of this church, or in this passageway, or upon these stones. To find yourself in the place, in the "here," where God's self-revelation unfolded can be supremely moving. Even the strongest of believers can find themselves with a profound new sense of the realness of the sacred events.

I certainly had my own *hic* moments during my time in Bethlehem, where my patient and gracious host family lived. They guided me to the popular and not-so-popular holy places throughout the city. After the initial tours, I spent most of my days at my desk researching historical items or walking around the city trying to absorb the day-to-day reality of the Palestinian Christians.

On good mornings, I'd walk the two blocks from my host family's apartment to the Church of the Holy Nativity. I'd go down to the grotto of the church and pray in front of the spot where the Lord was born. I'd trace my fingers along the fourteen-pointed star that marked the spot.

Those fourteen points of the star represent the generations of waiting for the coming of the promised Messiah: the fourteen generations from Abraham to David, the fourteen generations from David to the Babylonian Exile, and the fourteen generations from the exile to the coming of the Christ. The fourteen-point star is a message of promises made and promises fulfilled; a symbol of God's faithfulness, in the events of the real world, to his people.

Although I was in Bethlehem for some time, every such morning at the grotto was like the first time. Each visit, I could hear my soul say, "It really happened. And it happened right here. God became a man for us. He became a man for me. He came to save us; he came to save *me*."

Not every Christian will be able to make such a pilgrimage and experience the *hic* moments in that direct, present way. But all of us are able, invited, and indeed called to deepen our understanding and conviction of the historicity of God's saving words and deeds. Not all believers will visit the Church of the Holy Nativity, but every believer can encounter and adore Jesus Christ in the creche of their homes. Not all believers will make it to the holy city Jerusalem and touch the stone on Mount Calvary or pray in front of the *Edicule*—the small chapel built over the site of Jesus' empty tomb, but every believer is summoned to recognize, meditate upon, and defend the historical reality of the Lord's passion, death, and resurrection.

Our faith *must* be grounded on the historicity of the gospel. It cannot stand merely upon the emotional satisfaction derived from uplifting, well-intentioned myths or fuzzy moral lessons. The gospel only has real power, is only worthy of our complete devotion, if it's connected to what God really said and did. Right here. *Hic.*

Have I fully realized the historical nature of the gospel? Do I study and seek to have a strong knowledge of the revelations of God? Do I ground my faith on the historical reality of the gospel and not my own sentimental or emotional fulfillment?

The Example of the Transfiguration

Amid the darkness of neo-mythologizing by sentimentalists and relativists, the truth of the gospel shines through as a stable and reliable light along our pilgrim way.

After turning back to the Lord Jesus, St. Peter was steadfast in his apostolic ministry and heroically died a martyr for the Faith. As he was nearing his end, he turned the attention of believers to the historical and true reality of the gospel:

> Therefore I intend to keep on reminding you of these things, though you know them already and are established in the truth that has come to you. I think it right, as long as I am in this body, to refresh your memory, since I know that my death will come soon, as indeed our Lord Jesus Christ has made clear to me. And I will make every effort so that after my departure you

may be able at any time to recall these things (2 Pet. 1:12–15).

As his own crucifixion approached, he did not let fear and anxiety take his heart but grounded himself on the truth of the gospel, turning his whole attention to the historical event of the Transfiguration:

> For we did not follow cleverly devised myths when we made known to you the power and coming of our Lord Jesus Christ, but we had been eyewitnesses of his majesty. For he received honor and glory from God the Father when that voice was conveyed to him by the Majestic Glory, saying, "This is my Son, my Beloved, with whom I am well pleased." We ourselves heard this voice come from heaven, while we were with him on the holy mountain. So we have the prophetic message more fully confirmed. You will do well to be attentive to this as to a lamp shining in a dark place, until the day dawns and the morning star rises in your hearts (2 Pet. 1:16–19).

The chief apostle tells us, "We had been eyewitnesses," and "We ourselves heard," "while we were with him," and consequently "we have the prophetic message more fully confirmed." And as he was doing in his own life, Peter exhorts us to "be attentive to this [the prophetic message] as to a lamp shining in a dark place, until," he stresses with paternal affection, "the day dawns and the morning star rises in your hearts."

As the early Church denounced and dismissed "cleverly devised myths," so we are called to avoid self-styled versions of the true God and true gospel, holding instead to the full prophetic message as really seen, heard, and confirmed by eyewitnesses.

Do I allow my emotions or wishful thinking to change the gospel? Do I attempt to change the gospel because of the moral demands that flow from its historical and doctrinal realities? Do I steadfastly cling to the Lord Jesus in order to work out my salvation in him?

Application to Our Lives

Declarations of Discipleship

- I acknowledge the gospel as the true revelation of God to humanity, as completed and fulfilled in Jesus Christ.

- I believe in the historical reality of the gospel.

- I will not indulge in our contemporary versions of cleverly devised myths that deny or diminish the truth of the gospel.

Examination of Conscience

- Do I acknowledge the historical nature of the gospel?

- Do I order my life by the truths of the gospel?

- Do I understand my own historical reality and realize my decisions have real and eternal consequences?

- Am I preparing myself for judgment and eternal life?

- Do I avoid any mythical or fantastical thinking when it comes to the gospel?

- Do I actively avoid compromising the gospel in any way?

- Do I stay vigilant and dismiss any attempt of my fallen mind to create my own myths?

- Do I avoid the cultural and societal myths that are imposed on the gospel?

- Do I speak of Jesus Christ in the singular and refuse any syncretism of the gospel with lies and myths?

- Do I refrain from ideologies that seek to re-create mythical versions of God or Jesus Christ?

When you have made this examination of conscience, I recommend that you go and make a good confession based on these points.

Key Points

Here are some points to remember when speaking to others about the real, historical nature of Christianity:

1. The *gospel* ("good news") refers to the story of the life and teachings of Jesus; and in a broader sense we might refer to the full collection of God's true revelations, culminating in Jesus, as the gospel.

2. The gospel is historical and real.

3. Jesus Christ is a real person, fully human and fully divine, who brought redemption to humanity by his saving passion, death, and resurrection.

4. The gospel is true and does not contain any myths or mere moral lessons.

5. Myths are not restricted to the ancient world or primitive peoples.

6. Today there are many cultural and ideological myths about God and Jesus Christ.

7. Our fallen minds and hearts are inclined to make the gospel a myth so that free license can be given to our preferences and desires.

8. All cleverly devised myths hurt the integrity and credibility of the true gospel.

9. Believers must avoid myths in their own hearts and reject them in our culture.

Devotional Exercise

Prayer to the Holy Spirit (St. Augustine)

Breathe into me, Holy Spirit,
that my thoughts may all be holy.
Move in me, Holy Spirit,
that my work, too, may be holy.
Attract my heart, Holy Spirit,
that I may love only what is holy.
Strengthen me, Holy Spirit,
that I may defend all that is holy.

Protect me, Holy Spirit,
that I may always be holy.
Amen.

Act of Hope

O my God, relying on your almighty power and infinite mercy and promises, I hope to obtain pardon of my sins, the help of your grace, and life everlasting, through the merits of Jesus Christ, my Lord and Redeemer. Amen.

Prayer for Wisdom (St. Thomas Aquinas)

Give me, Lord God, a watchful heart, that no stray thought might distract me from you.

Give me a noble heart, that no unworthy affection might pull me down.

Give me a just heart that will not be divided by any dark intention.

Give me a strong heart that will not be broken by any tribulation.

Give me a free heart that will not follow any violent desire.

Give me, Lord God, a mind to know you, diligence to seek you, wisdom to find you, a life to please you, perseverance to wait faithfully for you, and the trust that will finally embrace you.

Amen.

Stations of the Cross

As you pray the stations of the cross, ask for the grace to avoid the myths and manipulations of the gospel in our day. In particular, focus on the fifth station, in which Simon of Cyrene carries the cross for the Lord Jesus.

Reflect on Jesus' desire to help you carry your own cross and receive its graces: "And they compelled a passer-by, Simon of Cyrene, who was coming in from the country, the father of Alexander and Rufus, to carry his cross" (Mark 15:21).

Rosary Suggestions

When praying the mysteries of the rosary, consider these points:

Joyful Mysteries: The historical nature of these events and the desire of the Son of God to come among us and offer us eternal life.

Luminous Mysteries: The historical nature of these events and the love of Jesus Christ for the Father as he lived a true, historical human life, loving others and serving others.

Sorrowful Mysteries: The historical nature of these events and the willingness of Jesus Christ to offer himself as a sacrifice for our salvation. Consider his faithfulness to the Father even amid torture and sufferings.

Glorious Mysteries: The true reality of eternal life that is offered to each of us in Jesus Christ.

CHAPTER THREE

THE WAY OF THE LORD, NOT OUR OWN WAY

I will meditate on all your work
and muse on your mighty deeds.
Your way, O God, is holy.
What god is so great as our God?

—Psalm 77:12–13

A few years ago, I was asked to be a part of a family's conversation on whether a recent in-law should become a Catholic. In the conversation, the woman in question—whom we'll call "Monica"—was defiantly opposed to the Church's teachings on artificial contraception, thought abortion was okay "in certain situations," and wasn't quite convinced about the whole "Communion thing."

I was surprised by the nature of the conversation and couldn't imagine why the family was pressuring Monica to become a Catholic.

As the conversation went back and forth, some of the family members' responses revealed more than they realized about their own discipleship, as they waffled on each of Monica's challenges:

It doesn't matter about contraception. You just have to decide what's best for your family...

Abortion is a tough one. But here's some wiggle room...

Yeah, the whole Body and Blood thing is confusing. The important part is that you feel Jesus is with you...

It was a sad example of how easy it is for Christians to dumb down God's truth and soften the demands of discipleship.

While listening to the conversation and trying to pray, I was eventually dragged in from the sidelines when one family member said to me, "Father, help us here. Isn't it just better if we're all of the same faith?" I tried not to smile as, according to the comments already made, oneness in faith seemed to be lacking around the room, and the plea continued: "The important thing is that Monica convert and become a Catholic. It's just good for families to share the same religion. Wouldn't you agree?"

I nodded at the person's words since there were semblances of truth in them, but there needed to be some clarification and correction. And so, sitting there in the family's living room and trying to respect my duties as their guest, I began:

"It *is* good for families to be united in faith, but faith has to be real. Faith is not a conviction in our own talents or decisions, but an overwhelming trust in the truth and providence of God. By *truth*, I mean objective facts about reality, whether about the things of this world or the world to come. By *providence*, I mean God's fatherly care for each of us.

"We have faith in things that are *real*," I continued. "This demands a certain death to ourselves..."

I paused. At this point, I could see family members reaching for snacks on the table and a diminishing of interest as they were wondering just where I was going in my end of the conversation. I had been brought in as the team mascot, to rally the cause and tell Monica to become Catholic. Mascots aren't supposed to have their own thoughts and they're not supposed to rock the boat.

But a Catholic priest is not a mascot. The Church is not a team. And discipleship is not a sport or a tribal association. I started again:

"Faith is about encountering God, receiving his public revelations, and hearing the call to reciprocate his love and to follow his divine Son, Jesus Christ, in working out our salvation. Faith leads to and requires *discipleship*. And discipleship is foremost about following the way of the Lord, not our own way. It means hearing the Lord Jesus speak and trusting him. It means accepting his teachings and surrendering to his way, mediated through the Church.

"At the end of the Order of Christian Initiation of Adults (OCIA), a person will be asked, 'Do you believe and profess *all* that the holy Catholic Church believes, teaches, and proclaims to be revealed by God?' If a person—from the depths of his conscience—cannot honestly say 'yes,' then he should wait. Such a time of waiting can be filled with sacred study, mentoring, prayer, holy fellowship with believers, and an overall desire to receive and integrate the graces of conversion, so that the question asked before God and the Church can ultimately be answered in the affirmative with his whole heart."

At this point, a different family member piped in, "Dang, Father. It sounds like you don't want Monica to become Catholic!"

"Oh, not true," I responded, "I greatly want Monica to become a Catholic Christian and to know the depth and the fullness of our faith, just as a greatly want each of you to go deeper and to know the same depth and fullness of our faith.

"Our faith is not a club. We're not 'Catholic, Inc.' We are the living Body of Christ, the People of God, who are bound to God by the New and Everlasting Covenant of Jesus Christ. It is a covenant expressed in a faithful following of the Lord's own way. Our faith is not an investment in ourselves or even in our family. Our faith is an investment in the way of the Lord Jesus."

"But not everyone's perfect, Father. We can't be a city of saints, otherwise only saints would feel comfortable with us," said another family member—the one who had earlier bragged about his Jesuit education and was firmly in support "of married people discerning for themselves whether contraception fits into their family planning."

"Yes, that's a great point," I said. "Even though we all want to become saints—since everyone in heaven is a saint—we are a city of sinners in this world. But as sinners who want to become saints, we don't wallow our sin. We don't justify or rationalize or become comfortable in our imperfections of belief or behavior.

"Instead, we repent and seek the grace of God for the transformation of our minds and the conversion of our hearts. When we don't fully believe something, we take a posture of docility and teachability. We seek the grace to come to deeper faith. We don't rebel or reject truths that are given to us. When we aren't living as were called to as the children of God, we repent and seek the graces of fortitude and perseverance. We seek constantly to be shaped and molded by the grace of God.

"The way of the Lord Jesus is a journey. There is no plateau. No pause. No resting on the status quo. We are works in progress and the Lord is constantly calling out to us, 'Come, follow me'" (Matt. 4:19).

Sensing it was time to wrap things up, and since the conversation was supposed to be for her, I addressed Monica directly:

"Monica, I want you to become a Catholic Christian, but only when you're ready. And you'll know when you're ready when you are comfortable with not deciding all the answers for yourself. Then you can be a *disciple*, taught and formed wholly and authentically in the way of the Lord Jesus."

Shortly after these comments, the conversation came to a gracious conclusion and I was kindly shown to the door. I would have enjoyed being a fly on the wall after I left as the family most likely sought to dismiss me as a zealot, and convince poor Monica that she really should just become the newest compromised member of the Catholic Church.

In the early Church, such halfway discipleship would have been rightly called out as no discipleship at all. The early followers of the Lord Jesus understood discipleship as *self-sacrifice,* necessary for the working-out of our salvation in Jesus Christ and a means of sharing in the glory of God. St. Paul summarized this understanding:

> For through the law I died to the law, so that I might live to God. I have been crucified with Christ; and it is no longer I who live, but it is

Christ who lives in me. And the life I now live in the flesh I live by faith in the Son of God, who loved me and gave himself for me (Gal. 2:19–20).

In my life, do I trust in the goodness and providence of God? Do I make the act of faith and seek to sacrificially follow the way of the Lord? When I struggle with sacred teachings or with virtue, do I humble myself and seek the help of God's grace?

Friendship Along the Way

After I was ordained a priest, my first assignment was to a circuit of parishes that included a large university. Since I arrived for my assignment in July, I was able to meet several of the summer students, international students who had come early, and some of the students who were on leadership teams organizing fall orientation.

Among these groups of students was a young man from Iran. He was a person of deep faith. I was humbled by the esteem he showed to my priesthood. At different times, he would stop by the parish office and give me updates on his academic work and his new life in the United States.

After the fall semester began, this student reached out to me in great perplexity. I made time to see him as quickly as possible, thinking it was some emergency with his family overseas. When we met, the young man was in tears. It took him a few minutes to compose himself and start talking. In time, he recounted his dismay with some of his university classmates. Over the summer, a small group of them had hung out together, discussed family things, shared fears and hopes, played sports, eaten meals, and become good friends. But when the fall semester began, those new friends were suddenly too busy for him.

Those students had approached their Iranian class-mate's friendship the way many modern people do. It was casual, situational, and transient. There was no commitment or faithfulness in their understanding of friendship. The Iranian young man, however, approached friendship as an extension of family. He was offering his heart, loyalty, and devotion. And his heart was broken when his new Western friends were bored, distracted, or busy being entertained by others.

This experience helps to give us a context for the biblical understanding of friendship. The young man's notion of friendship hearkens back to the profound notion of friendship that we find in the sacred scriptures.

The Lord Jesus offers us his friendship and in so doing provides a model for friendship:

> This is my commandment, that you love one another as I have loved you. No one has greater love than this, to lay down one's life for one's friends. You are my friends if you do what I command you. I do not call you servants any longer, because the servant does not know what the master is doing; but I have called you friends, because I have made known to you everything that I have heard from my Father. You did not choose me but I chose you. And I appointed you to go and bear fruit, fruit that will last, so that the Father will give you whatever you ask him in my name. I am giving you these commands so that you may love one another (John 15:12–17).

In contrast to this example, too often our culture treats friendship cheaply and pollutes it with utilitarianism and sentimental self-absorption. We seek out our friends when we want something from them. We use people and expect them to entertain us. We demand that our friends be low maintenance, or else we just avoid them. Lacking depth and substance, we see friendship as fleeting and inconsequential.

But the biblical understanding of friendship is rich in love and commitment. When the Lord offers us his friendship, he is offering us his brotherhood and the exalted status as adopted children of God. Such a friendship is to be treasured, honored, protected, and nurtured.

The Lord's friendship is not cold or self-serving, but an encouraging friendship where heart speaks to heart. It is a friendship of companions and confidants who accompany one another and walk together through the trials, sorrows, and joys of life.

Our friendship with the Lord Jesus, moreover, is not something we *merit* or *deserve*. It is not something we can demand as if it were our right. It is a gift given to us. As such, our friendship with the Lord should be marked by a clinging, grasping, and holding-tight to the Lord as we walk his way and seek out our salvation in him. We're not doing Jesus a favor by being his friend! He does not need us. He gains nothing in befriending us. He offers his friendship out of sheer, generous goodness. It is *we* who gain—who gain everything—by accepting his friendship and walking with him.

Do I realize the heartfelt depth of friendship? Do I understand friendship as a kind of familial relationship? Do I accept the Lord's friendship and actively seek to be a true and faithful friend to him?

Holy Drowning and New Life

The Lord Jesus initiates our friendship with him at our baptism. There are many images from the early Church that can help us understand the interior transformation that occurs in baptism and the radical call to discipleship it places within our souls. One of the more popular (and perhaps startling) images was the notion of the *holy drowning*. Baptism was a drowning—a dying—in the Lord Jesus.

As a help to grasping this provocative notion, imagine the following situation:

You and some of your closest friends are aboard a large boat on the ocean. You're relaxed and enjoying a gentle breeze and a cold drink. You're standing by the edge of the boat and casually moving to some music. All of a sudden, you hear a noise in the water behind you. You can tell from the faces of the people in front of you that something is not right.

Something suddenly grabs you from behind. *Boom!* And throws you over the boat. *Splash!* You hit the water and are shocked. Once you gain your bearings, you begin to fight to break free of what feels like a strong current, but to no avail. You seem powerless. You can see the boat getting farther and farther away from you.

Eventually, you're able to maneuver yourself and look behind you. You're shocked when you realize that it's not a current holding you, but Jesus. You scream over the waves, "Let me go, I'm drowning. I'm dying. Let me go!" He tells you to trust him. He calls you to surrender.

You stop struggling and resign yourself to his goodness and kindness, even if it pulls you under the sea. The moment you yield to him, he squeezes you and together you skyrocket out of the water and seem to be floating in the air. You experience for a moment the glory of the resurrection. You have drowned and have been saved. You died and then were reborn from on high. You are no longer your own; you are now united to Jesus Christ.

Welcome to the mysterious, mystical, and transformative waters of holy baptism!

For it is indeed only when we are willing to live and die by the baptismal waters that we are able to realize within ourselves the power and glory of the Lord's passion, death, and resurrection. This re-living of the paschal mystery is not mere symbolism or lofty theology. It is a walking with the Lord Jesus in the trenches of our lives, feeling the passion of temptation, sin, fear, and anxiety, dying to such darkness, and then living anew in Jesus Christ. When we die to ourselves, we are born to newness of life in him. There is no discipleship without dying in baptism, just as there is no discipleship without the cross.

As baptized Christians and members of Christ's own body, we are called to live by faith in Jesus Christ. As the Lord Jesus died and rose again, so we are called to die to ourselves and live anew in him.

St. Paul poses a question to the early Christians and to each of us:

> Do you know that all of us who have been baptized into Christ Jesus were baptized into his death? We were buried therefore with him by baptism into death, so that as Christ was raised from the dead by the glory of the Father, we too might walk in newness of life (Rom. 6:3–4).

Here Paul helps us to see the two paths before us. Later in this letter he juxtaposes two ways of living: "life according to the flesh" (meaning our fallen attraction to evil and pleasure, not simply having bodies) and "life according to the Spirit" (Rom. 8:3–13).

As baptized Christians seeking to follow the way of the Lord, we are enabled and empowered to live a life according to the Spirit and bear the fruits of the Spirit in our lives:

> By contrast, the fruit of the Spirit is love, joy, peace, patience, kindness, generosity, faithfulness, gentleness, and self-control. There is no law against such things. And those who belong to Christ Jesus have crucified the flesh with its passions and desires. If we live by the Spirit, let us also be guided by the Spirit. Let us not become conceited, competing against one another, envying one another (Gal. 5:22–26).

We are not children of darkness. We are not children of disorder. We are the children of God, adopted siblings of the Lord Jesus and temples of the Holy Spirit. As we die to ourselves, we live by the Spirit of our adoption.

Do I realize that in baptism I have died to myself? Do I surrender myself to the work of the Lord? Do I work to live a life according to the Spirit?

Salvation Through Suffering

Earlier in my priesthood, I pastorally ministered to a man who had cared for his adult son during his son's battle with cancer. As I came to know the man, he shared with me the account of his son's life and holy death. When the son was first diagnosed with cancer, no one realized how serious it was. As the medical team did more tests, it became clear that the cancer was terminal, and that the young man's physical life was nearing its end. In response to this news, the father told me, he retired early, merged savings and investments, and did everything he could do in order to accompany his son through his illness.

Before his son's cancer, the father said, he would have described his family as "a normal Catholic family." By that expression he meant they periodically went to Sunday Mass—but they didn't take the Faith too seriously. They didn't view life through a lens of God's providence. They practiced no personal dedication to Jesus Christ. They didn't make life decisions based on the truths of the Faith. There was little family prayer and no commitment to the local parish, and no real service to others outside of the family. Sadly, the father was right: his family was pretty "normal" among Catholics in Western culture today.

As the father sacrificed his career and accepted a simpler life, he rolled up his sleeves and cared for his son: giving shots, tracking medicines, adjusting meals, cleaning up vomit, changing adult diapers, cooperating with doctors and hospice workers, caressing his scared son and giving him the constancy and consolation of a father's love.

And as the cancer worsened, something else happened: the father's dormant faith woke up. He realized that an aspect of his son's care had been missing and that something *spiritual* needed to be done. Not knowing where to turn, he picked up the Bible and started reading the Gospel books to his son. As he read them, he was at once encouraged and shocked, comforted and unsettled—and inspired to greater faith. He hadn't realized who Jesus was and what he was calling us to do.

This made the father somewhat angry, in fact, because he felt that no one had preached this gospel to him or challenged him or his family to live by it.

As the father was telling me his experience, he told me that while he was reading the Gospels he felt an overwhelming new conviction, brought on by a few simple questions that were whispered into his soul: *What if Jesus meant what he said? What if salvation is something we must really work on? What's going to happen to my son after he dies?*

Everything was different from that point. The father arranged for confession for the entire family and for the anointing of the sick for his son. He asked for Holy Communion to be brought to his son on a regular basis. He started praying with his son and family, and he admitted to me how hard it was to do at first, wondering, "Why was it hard to pray with my family? They're the most important people to me in my entire life." Slowly, he evicted the secularism that had invaded his home. He spoke about the Lord Jesus with his family, the hospice workers, and even a few delivery guys. He looked for ways to show patience and kindness, and started donating to the poor. He began asking other people to pray for his son and promising to pray for their own intentions. He finished the Gospels and went on to read the rest of the New Testament to his son.

During this blessed time, the most difficult hurdle for the father was the conversation he needed to have with his son about redemptive suffering and death. No one in the family wanted to talk about his looming death, and certainly not with him. But finally, the father accepted this cross, sat down, and started talking with his son about dying and death. Together they cried holy tears.

There was a pause, and the son patted his father's head, buried in the blankets as he crouched alongside the bed, and told him, "Thanks, Dad . . . I'm glad we can talk about this."

But the conversation wasn't over. The father began to witness to his son. He repented for having been such a bad Christian in the son's youth and shared his zealous faith with him. The son laughed, and told him, "Yeah, I figured something happened. It's gotten a lot different around here." The father laughed too, and then told his son, "But, son, you have some really hard work to do. The Lord has given you a cross. I wish it were my cross, but he's given this one to you. And you need to embrace it and start carrying it. This is how you're called to follow the Lord right now. This is how you're going to get to heaven and help a lot of other people get there too."

Again they wept. "I'm not crying because you're going away and won't be here anymore," the father insisted. "I'm crying because I'll miss your smile, your hugs, and having you around. I'm crying because I won't be able to see you grow up or have children. I'm crying because I'll miss you. But I'm not crying because you'll be away or lost forever. I know you'll be with me, and I know we can be together, with your mom and sisters in eternal life, but we have to do our part. We need to accept the cross. Son, you need to do this work because I can't imagine heaven without you. This is very serious."

The father told me that his son was moved to repentance. He asked to see the priest again and began to offer up his pain and sufferings for his family, other people who were dying, the poor and hungry, those without a family, and for other intentions. The son allowed his death bed to become his Calvary, and a great share in redemption was accomplished through it.

When the hour came for the son's death, the father

told me, it was a holy death, even marked with the famed smell of roses.

Now, as the man finished his story, he told me, "I miss my son every day. Each day there's something that reminds me and my wife of him. I thought I wouldn't see his smile or feel his hug, but I see his smile in a dozen places, and I feel his hugs in a dozen others. I know he's with me. I especially feel him at the Mass. I call it our 'altar reunion.' I can't wait to see him face-to-face again. But I need to keep carrying my cross now and let the Lord make me ready."

This encounter has been one of the most life-changing and spiritually renewing experiences of my priesthood. I would think about it often, especially as I and my family ministered to my own father as he was dying and preparing for eternity.

Our Way of the Cross

The man's wise question should shake us: "What if Jesus meant what he said?" The Lord Jesus is calling us to the cross so that it can make us fit to be with him in his heavenly kingdom. There is no Christ without the cross. There is no heaven without the cross.

The Lord Jesus says to us (and he means it):

> If any want to become my followers, let them deny themselves and take up their cross and follow me. For those who want to save their life will lose it, and those who lose their life for my sake will find it. For what will it profit them if they gain the whole world but forfeit their life? Or what will they give in return for their life? (Matt. 16:24–26).

The way of the Lord Jesus is accepting the cross. The spiritual masters rightly teach us that we will either embrace the cross and move toward eternal life or be dragged by it and move toward eternal damnation.

Regrettably, though in contemporary Western Christian discipleship, the cross has become a trinket, mere religious imagery; a tame, sterilized symbol stripped of meaning. To rediscover its full meaning and thus to really understand the point Jesus was making when he called us to embrace our cross, we need to understand its historical context.

Crucifixion was invented hundreds of years before Christ by the Assyrians, considered one of the more bloodthirsty cultures in human history. It was subsequently used by the Babylonians and also favored among the Persians.

The Romans used the cross as a method of execution, but their sense of virtue made them cringe at its use. The Roman philosopher Cicero even said that no Roman should ever utter the word "cross" since it was so uncivilized and unbecoming to Rome's nobility. By imperial law, in fact, no Roman could be crucified; it was considered beneath the dignity of a citizen. Nevertheless, Rome used the cross as a means of domination and control among occupied peoples and nations.

Death by the cross was barbarous, humiliating, and excruciatingly savage—not a topic for polite conversation. When the Lord Jesus first called for his followers to take up *their* cross, then, the reaction must have been shocked disbelief. "Why is this Teacher saying such crazy things?" They would have been scared, confused, and offended by such an exhortation. The cross was the height of cruelty and humiliation. What could it possibly have to do with being a disciple?

But Jesus was not joking, or being figurative, or even exaggerating. The Lord tells us that in order to follow him we must be ready to accept pain, suffering, persecution, humiliation, and a death to our own desires. The cross, once a symbol of desolation, is transformed into a means of total self-abandonment and a declaration of complete confidence in the providence of God.

As a help to breaking down any nice, merely symbolic understanding of the cross, imagine the electric chair, which is still used in many parts of the United States for capital punishment. Imagine the strips of leather, the cords and wires, and the fear of being strapped into it knowing that enough electricity will be sent through your body that your hair will smoke, your blood will boil, and you will die. It is a horrible device.

The electric chair still does not even come close to the torture and brutality of death on the cross. But still, imagine the Lord Jesus saying to us today, "If you want to follow me, you must sit with me on the electric chair, and fry with me."

The invitation should unsettle us! We want comfort and ease. We want our autonomy and control. We want respectability and status. We don't want to suffer. And yet, the Lord Jesus is calling us to die to all our wants—to fry with him—and to live solely for him and his kingdom.

If anyone claims to be a disciple of the Lord but rejects the cross, such a person is a deceiver. The cross is the *standard* of our discipleship. It is the cost we pay to be made fit for eternal life.

Do I realize that the Lord Jesus meant what he said, and so embrace the cross when it's given to me? Do I denounce the false promises of comfort, status, and respectability? Do I let the cross discipline me and make us fit for the kingdom of God?

The Baptismal Way

As the son of a retired Army first sergeant, and as someone who has served in the military myself, I'm often invited onto military installations to give talks, conferences, and retreats. On one such occasion, the hosting chaplain was a war veteran and shared with me a powerful story relating to one of our wounded veterans.

The soldier in question was in Afghanistan, where his unit was responsible for patrolling a few towns. On one patrol, the unit was ambushed. The vehicle the soldier was in hit a land mine and the unit came under heavy fire. The soldier was knocked unconscious and did not wake up until later in the hospital, having lost both his legs.

The chaplain was there as the wounded soldier came out of his coma. The young man asked where he was, and the chaplain told him he was in a hospital and that his unit had suffered an attack. Without a second thought, the soldier asked how his fellow soldiers were.

The chaplain avoided the question and told the young man, "I have some difficult news for you. In the attack, your vehicle hit a landmine. Son, I'm very sorry, but you lost both your legs."

The soldier had not yet realized this and, surprised, he looked down to see his legs missing. Then he looked up and, giving the chaplain a stern glare, said to him, "No, chaplain, I didn't lose my legs. I *gave* them!"

The story of a soldier giving his legs in defense of his nation gives us a context in which we can better understand our baptismal call to give our entire selves to the Lord Jesus Christ and his kingdom. The summons to die to ourselves is real and it's difficult. It requires an oblation, a complete giving of ourselves to the Lord.

The modern world is fueled by obsession with self. From social media's glorification of narcissism to the constant self-indulgence of consumerism, our culture's dominant messaging is that we are the center of the world and that we should be given whatever we want, when we want it, and however we want it. If we are not constantly vigilant, we can find ourselves warped by these messages, convinced of the sovereignty of Self. If we are not attentive, we begin to indulge in our culture's radical subjectivism, convinced little by little that our preferred way of life is more important than any other—even the way of the Lord Jesus.

Such thoughts are disastrous to authentic Christian discipleship. In place of the Father, Son, and Holy Spirit, we begin to worship the false Trinity of me, myself, and I, along with that god's fallen way of comfort, status, and respectability. We zealously pursue a "bucket list" of vain worldly goals as if eternal life did not even exist.

In the midst of such intoxicating distraction, our task is to discern the way of the Lord; to choose it intentionally, watch it diligently, and follow it earnestly. It is so easy to lose sight of the mark, lose our way, and find ourselves compromised—lukewarm, claiming to be a disciple when in reality we are mostly the Lord's fair-weather friends.

We know this about ourselves, don't we? We do not think, speak, or act as we ought. We are not complete in ourselves. But the good news is that *God makes us complete.* We have the sure way of the Lord Jesus to teach, train, correct, encourage, admonish, and console us so that we can work out our salvation in him. We have the active power of God's grace and the guidance of the gospel and the Church to put us back on the path when we stray from God's friendship. When Paul gives us the summons

to discipleship, he assures us that it includes *transforma-*
tion from the weakness of our sinful selves and with it a
greater discernment of the Lord's way:

> I appeal to you therefore, brothers and sisters,
> by the mercies of God, to present your bodies
> as a living sacrifice, holy and acceptable to God,
> which is your spiritual worship. Do not be con-
> formed to this world, but be transformed by the
> renewing of your minds, so that you may dis-
> cern what is the will of God—what is good and
> acceptable and perfect (Rom. 12:1–2).

And so, as members of the baptized who have died to
ourselves that we might live more fully in Jesus Christ,
we are compelled by faith to constantly choose the way of
the Lord Jesus above our own way, above the ways of our
fallen world, above the ways proposed by sin, self-centeredness, and a desire for worldly respect.

The baptismal way of life is taught and expressed in
the ancient *baptismal promises*. In the first three promises
we denounce sin, the wayward attraction to sin, and Satan. In the last three promises we acknowledge our faith
in the Holy Trinity: Father, Son, and Holy Spirit. In
summary fashion, these promises express the biblical and
patristic teachings on the baptismal way of life. And, although they were developed theologically over time, in
their basic form the baptismal promises come to us from
the early Church.

The baptismal promises show how clearly the early
Church understood baptism and how our forefathers and
foremothers clung to the graces of baptism, readily accepting its call to faithfully and selflessly follow the way
of the Lord Jesus.

Baptismal Promises

Do you renounce sin,
    so as to live in the freedom of the children
    of God?

Do you reject the lure of evil,
    so that sin may have no mastery over you?

Do you reject Satan,
    the author and prince of sin?

Do you believe in God,
    the Father almighty, Creator of heaven and
    earth?

Do you believe in Jesus Christ,
    his only Son, our Lord, who was born of
    the Virgin Mary, suffered death and was
    buried, rose again from the dead, and is
    seated at the right hand of the Father?

Do you believe in the Holy Spirit,
    the holy Catholic Church, the communion
    of saints, the forgiveness of sins, the resur-
    rection of the body, and life everlasting?

Do I understand the personal and eternal significance of my baptism? Do I live the baptismal way of life? Do I regularly review the baptismal promises and ask for the graces to faithfully love and serve God?

Followers of the Way

When the Lord Jesus began his public ministry, he preached a simple yet compelling message: "Repent, for the kingdom of heaven has come near" (Matt. 4:17). This hearkening was followed by the invitation: "Come, follow me." This summons was not symbolic or figurative. It was not an emblem nor an allegory. The Lord Jesus was seriously and literally calling people to *follow* him, which involved the major sacrifice of leaving their homes, families, work, and towns.

Today, discipleship has been smothered with symbolic language, making such a literal and practical application of Jesus' first call startling to us. Of course, following Jesus today isn't quite so literal—walking behind an itinerant rabbi as he journeys and teaches and performs miracles—yet we have nonetheless cushioned the grit of discipleship, turned it into a relaxing, comfortable way of life. We have inverted the call of discipleship, focusing on its rewards and viewing its sacrifices with suspicion and derision.

The Lord Jesus corrects this in no uncertain terms:

> Now large crowds were traveling with him; and he turned and said to them, "Whoever comes to me and does not hate father and mother, wife and children, brothers and sisters, yes, and even life itself, cannot be my disciple. Whoever does not carry the cross and follow me cannot be my disciple" (Luke 14:25–27).

And, when some wanted to apply conditions to their response, the Lord was unrelenting in his expectations:

As they were going along the road, someone said to him, "I will follow you wherever you go." And Jesus said to him, "Foxes have holes, and birds of the air have nests; but the Son of Man has nowhere to lay his head." To another he said, "Follow me." But he said, "Lord, first let me go and bury my father." But Jesus said to him, "Let the dead bury their own dead; but as for you, go and proclaim the kingdom of God." Another said, "I will follow you, Lord; but let me first say farewell to those at my home." Jesus said to him, "No one who puts a hand to the plow and looks back is fit for the kingdom of God" (Luke 9:57–62).

To any person who said he wanted to be a disciple but was unwilling to leave everything and follow after him, the Lord was equally clear:

Whoever loves father or mother more than me is not worthy of me; and whoever loves son or daughter more than me is not worthy of me; and whoever does not take up the cross and follow me is not worthy of me. Those who find their life will lose it, and those who lose their life for my sake will find it (Matt. 10:37–39).

In the course of time, discipleship became stational. (Although the early bishops, as successors of the apostles, retained the original call of discipleship and to this day remain "on the go," as witnesses to the truth that, as Christians, we are to be in the world but never of it.) Yet although our discipleship is not itinerant, we must not try to "shelter in place" in the world. This passing, fallen world is not our home and we should never feel fully safe or at home in its comforts, luxuries, and false peace. We must reject worldly ideologies that are contrary to the goodness of God and his plan of authentic love and salvation. We must pursue a life of holiness, guard our virtues, and not permit ourselves to be held in the grip of sin, and vice.

And so, although most of us do not *literally* abandon everything in our discipleship today, we are called to be spiritually detached from this world, to live *as if* we do. And then, should the times demand it, to be prepared to make the more drastic and literal sacrifice of our possessions, family, and lives for the sake of the kingdom.

The context of early discipleship can serve as a litmus test for us. What would hold us back if we were called to literally leave everything and walk with the Lord? In that light, what is holding us back *now* as we are called to give everything to the Lord? The context of early discipleship can provoke us, humble us, and lead us to a sobering examination of conscience. Are we faithfully living and following the way of the Lord Jesus, pursuing a life of detachment, simplicity, and a holy indifference to the things of this world?

In the early Church, the disciples of the Lord Jesus came to be called "followers of the Way." They did not consider themselves worthy to be called "Christian," which means "little Christ." They followed the Lord's way and saw it as an apt summary of who they were and what they were actually doing—journeying with the Lord Jesus.

The term *way* also reflected adherence to the teachings of the Lord Jesus, as he taught us: "Jesus said to him, 'I am the way, and the truth, and the life. No one comes to the Father except through me'" (John 14:6). In the Christian community, that meant living, loving, and serving as the Lord himself lived, loved, and served, committing to the doctrines and worship handed on through the apostles: "They devoted themselves to the apostles' teaching and fellowship, to the breaking of bread and the prayers" (Acts 2:42).

In the entire New Testament, the name *Christian* was used in an extremely limited manner. But references to the "way" can be found throughout the scriptural accounts of the very early Church:

- Before his conversion, Paul sought to persecute the early Church. We're told that he received permission to imprison anyone who "belonged to the Way" (Acts 9:2; 22:4).

- On one occasion in Paul's missionary travels, he was harassed by a bad spirit that deplored the "way of salvation" that the apostle was living and teaching:

  One day, as we were going to the place of prayer, we met a slave-girl who had a spirit of divination and brought her owners a great deal of money by fortune-telling. While she followed Paul and us, she would cry out, "These men are slaves of the Most High God, who proclaim to you a way of salvation." She kept doing this for many days. But Paul, very much annoyed, turned and said to the spirit, "I order you in the name of Jesus Christ to come out of her." And it came out that very hour (Acts 16:16–18).

- The holy couple Priscilla and Aquila, who were teachers of the faith and very dear to Paul, spoke of the "way of God" as they give correction and instruction to Apollos (Acts 18:26).

- When St. Paul was brought before the governor Felix, the apostle to the Gentiles, appealed to the "the Way" and told the imperial authority:

  > But this I admit to you, that according to the Way, which they call a sect, I worship the God of our ancestors, believing everything laid down according to the law or written in the prophets (Acts 24:14).

- St. Peter, the chief apostle, teaches about "the way of truth" (2 Pet. 2:2).

- The author of the Letter to the Hebrews dramatically calls the body of the Lord Jesus "the new and living way" as he gives a description of the life of the early Church:

  > Therefore, my friends, since we have confidence to enter the sanctuary by the blood of Jesus, by the new and living way that he opened for us through the curtain (that is, through his flesh), and since we have a great priest over the house of God, let us approach with a true heart in full assurance of faith, with our hearts sprinkled clean from an evil conscience and our bodies washed with pure water. Let us hold fast to the confession of our hope without wavering, for he who has promised is faithful. And let us consider how to provoke one an-

> other to love and good deeds, not neglecting
> to meet together, as is the habit of some, but
> encouraging one another, and all the more as
> you see the Day approaching (Heb. 10:19–25).

Followers emphasizes the dynamic, spirited, and vigorous relationship that the Lord's disciples have with him. *The way* stresses the journey and accompaniment that disciples share with their Savior and Lord. Together, the expression highlights the creative momentum toward the holiness of God that is born from trusting and unconditionally loving the Lord Jesus in all we say and do.

Imagine the anticipation and suspense of the apostles every morning as they woke up and wondered, "What is the Lord going to do today?" They witnessed his signs and wonders. They heard his prophetic preaching, were edified by his wisdom and moved by his conviction and compassion. The apostles glimpsed the power of the Lord as he brought sight back to the blind, hearing to the deaf, restoration to the impaired, and hope to the desolate.

Truly, every day was an adventure. Every day with the Lord Jesus was a trek. The apostles never knew what the Master would do or say. They simply followed him and sought to learn from him, receive his grace, live his way, love with his heart, and spread his kingdom. They were his disciples; they *followed* him.

It was likely unbelievers, from the outside looking in, who first called these disciples "Christians." We read in the Acts of the Apostles,

> Then Barnabas went to Tarsus to look for Saul,
> and when he had found him, he brought him to
> Antioch. So it was that for an entire year they
> met with the church and taught a great many

people, and it was in Antioch that the disciples were first called "Christians" (Acts 11:25–26).

We can imagine the term being used in an almost derogatory manner, as if to say, "Look at those foolish 'Christians!' What are they doing among the sick? Why are they so narrow-minded in their beliefs that they're accepting persecution?"

That passage is one of only three uses of the term *Christian* in the entire New Testament. The second comes from the mouth of King Agrippa of Judea. He was a Jewish believer and was examining Paul, who had been brought to him for trial. In the exchange, the apostle challenges the king.

> King Agrippa, do you believe the prophets? I know that you believe." Agrippa said to Paul, "Are you so quickly persuading me to become a Christian?" Paul replied, "Whether quickly or not, I pray to God that not only you but also all who are listening to me today might become such as I am—except for these chains" (Acts 26:27–29).

It is interesting to note that Paul does not reciprocally use the term. Instead, the apostle simply says that he hopes the king and all his listeners "might become such as I am."

With this same understanding, Peter gives us the third and final use of the name *Christian*—indicating that those who are Christian are those who are *persecuted*. Something about the manner of life exhibited by the followers of Jesus' way provokes a violent response from the world. The "followers of the Way" did not follow Roman ways.

They refused to participate in the public games, the bac-
chanalia, and other expressions of violence, obscenity,
and moral licentiousness. This confused and offended the
Romans, who expected conformity with their way and
their gods.

It was for this reason that the Emperor Nero found
in the Christians an easy scapegoat for the Great Fire of
A.D. 64, when the majority of the Eternal City burned
to the ground. Nero could easily blame "the Christians"
for such arson since they had supposedly angered the gods
of Rome and the people already detested them and their
way of life.

In reply to such persecution, Peter uses the name *Christian* and writes,

> If you are reviled for the name of Christ, you are
> blessed, because the spirit of glory, which is the
> Spirit of God, is resting on you. But let none of
> you suffer as a murderer, a thief, a criminal, or
> even as a mischief maker. Yet if any of you suf-
> fers as a Christian, do not consider it a disgrace,
> but glorify God because you bear this name. For
> the time has come for judgment to begin with
> the household of God; if it begins with us, what
> will be the end for those who do not obey the
> gospel of God? (1 Pet. 4:14–17).

These are the three uses of the name *Christian* in the
New Testament. Each of them highlights something that
was viewed by outsiders as noteworthy about those who
were following Jesus' way.

Although Jesus' disciples soon embraced that name and
do so to this day, it is profitable to retain the initial sense
of *the Way*, of the name by which our spiritual forefathers

and foremothers in the Faith identified themselves. Though we now call ourselves "Christians," we can still spiritually retrieve and preserve the original dynamism and zeal of being a follower of and traveler on a way. In so doing, we can avoid becoming stagnant or stuck in a compromised version of what it means to be a disciple of Jesus. We are on the way. Our discipleship is a journey toward heaven and we confidently walk with our Lord.

Have I become attached to the things of this world? Have I become encumbered by the comforts and luxuries of life? Do I seek to live our lives on the way, constantly desiring continuous conversion to the Lord Jesus?

Rekindling the Gift of God

Using the power of our imagination within our own souls, we can mentally compose the encounter of the Lord Jesus with his first apostles. We can see the sun beaming off the waters of the Sea of Galilee, we can hear the noise of the water's movement and the birds flying above, we can taste the dust of the shore filling the air, we can smell the fish and barnacles, and we can touch the warm water and the stones along the water's edge. Having this place before us, we can see the Lord there on the shores of Galilee:

> As he walked by the Sea of Galilee, he saw two brothers, Simon, who is called Peter, and Andrew his brother, casting a net into the sea—for they were fishermen. And he said to them, "Follow me, and I will make you fish for people." Immediately they left their nets and followed him. As he went from there, he saw two other brothers, James son of Zebedee and his brother

John, in the boat with their father Zebedee, mending their nets, and he called them. Immediately they left the boat and their father, and followed him (Matt. 4:18–22).

With this composition of place, we can also see the Lord Jesus on the shores of our heart. We can hear his sacred voice call out to us. We sense his piercing eyes and feel the power of his gaze within our own souls. We hear him say, "Come, follow me!"

As baptized Christians, we have been chosen by Jesus Christ:

> You did not choose me, but I chose you. And I appointed you to go and bear fruit, fruit that will last, so that the Father will give you whatever you ask him in my name (John 15:16).

As we have been chosen, we are called and guided by grace to choose him, willingly and joyfully, and to faithfully follow his way. Such a summons demands our entire lives! And so we must constantly "rekindle the gift of God" that has been given to us (see 2 Tim. 1:6).

As a part of the process of rekindling the gift of God within us, of fanning his gift into a flame, we are called to make a *personal decision* for Jesus Christ. The Lord Jesus invites us every day, "Come, follow me!" and we are invited to give a definitive and continual "yes" to him, every day.

As those who have received the holy drowning and been baptized into Jesus Christ, we need to make and renew in our own hearts a personal decision for Jesus Christ. We need to seek a constant process of conversion, of a continual turning-toward and trusting of the Lord

Jesus in all we say and do. We are never "done" in our discipleship—not in this life. On earth there is no status quo, no plateau; there is only the journey—the way of the Lord—and the constant process of renewal that comes with it.

Listen to how the Second Vatican Council, in its Decree on Missionary Activity, describes the conversion of the non-believer (and by extension the conversion that should daily happen within the one who believes):

> This conversion must be taken as an initial one, yet sufficient to make a man realize that he has been snatched away from sin and led into the mystery of God's love, who called him to enter into a personal relationship with him in Christ. For, by divine grace, the new convert sets out on a spiritual journey, by means of which, already sharing through faith in the mystery of Christ's death and resurrection, he passes from the old man to the new one, perfected in Christ (*Ad Gentes* 13).

Pope St. John Paul II stressed this same point as he taught us:

> From the outset, conversion is expressed in faith which is total and radical, and which neither limits nor hinders God's gift. At the same time, it gives rise to a dynamic and lifelong process which demands a continual turning away from "life according to the flesh" to "life according to the Spirit" (cf. Rom. 8:3–13). Conversion means accepting, by a personal decision, the saving

sovereignty of Christ and becoming his disciple (*Redemptoris Missio* 46).

As baptized Christians and followers of Christ's way, we must allow the grace of God to actively work within us, and by it to make a robust personal commitment in our own lives—a declaration—that "Jesus Christ is Lord" (Phil. 2:11). Not simply acknowledging that Jesus is, objectively, the Lord of all—which he is—but also subjectively declaring him to be *our* Lord, the Lord of *my* life.

We are invited to make the intentional decision to abandon the "life according to the flesh" and actively and energetically choose "life according to the Spirit." We must also be able to believe, say, and every day let our souls grow in the conviction that, as Paul put it in Galatians 2:20, Jesus Christ "loved me and gave himself for me."

Only by such a personal, existential, wholehearted, and completely free decision in the depths of our being can we truly accept the love of the Lord Jesus, work to reciprocate his love as best as we are able, die to ourselves and our preferences and desires, and zealously and faithfully live out our baptismal graces in order to follow his way above all others.

As John Paul II said,

> Faith is a decision involving one's whole existence. It is an encounter, a dialogue, a communion of love and life between the believer and Jesus Christ, the Way, and the Truth, and the Life (cf. John 14:6). It entails an act of trusting abandonment to Christ, which enables us to live as he lived (cf. Gal. 2:20), in profound love of God and of our brothers and sisters (*Veritatis Splendor* 88).

Our discipleship is deepened, and the gift of God is
rekindled within us, when we make and continuously renew a personal decision for Jesus Christ—and then zealously work to stick to that decision by following his way.

At times, however, any disciple can slip, take a wayward detour, and lose his way. In such moments, we can
be reminded of the instruction of the Lord Jesus to the
holy women: "Do not be afraid; go and tell my brothers
to go to Galilee; there they will see me" (Matt. 28:10).

The apostles had abandoned the Lord in his darkest
hour. They fled and denied him in his passion and death.
Now, the risen Christ in Jerusalem tells them to meet
him in Galilee. That region of Galilee was in the north,
a fair distance from the holy city. Why put them through
that journey?

Perhaps he summoned them to Galilee since that is
where they first met him, accepted his invitation to follow
him, and came to know and love him. The instruction to
travel to Galilee was thus a *call to repentance*—directions to
get back on the way.

St. John gives us that same direction when he admon-
ishes us all to return to our first love:

> I know your works, your toil and your patient
> endurance. I know that you cannot tolerate evil-
> doers; you have tested those who claim to be
> apostles but are not, and have found them to be
> false. I also know that you are enduring patiently
> and bearing up for the sake of my name, and
> that you have not grown weary. But I have this
> against you, that you have abandoned the love
> you had at first. Remember then from what you
> have fallen; repent, and do the works you did
> at first. If not, I will come to you and remove

your lampstand from its place, unless you repent (Rev. 2:2–5).

If we have strayed from the way of the Lord Jesus, or if our love for him has become lukewarm, or if we realize that we have become compromised and attached to fallen things, then we also are invited to go to Galilee and return to the love we had at first. We are given the opportunity to renew our love for the Lord, convert back to him, and recommit ourselves to his lordship and to following his most excellent way.

Have I fanned my baptism into flame and made a personal decision for Jesus Christ? Do I seek to follow the way of the Lord and allow it to shape and mold my entire life, including the way I show mercy, spend money, plan out family life, vote, serve the poor, and protect the vulnerable and weak? Am I open to the graces of continual conversion in all I do and say?

The Context of the Rich Young Man

The context for such a personal decision for Jesus Christ is given to us in the encounter between the Lord Jesus and the Rich Young Man. The dialogue between the two is contained in the three Synoptic Gospels of Matthew, Mark, and Luke (Matt. 19:16–22; Mark 10:17–22; Luke 18:18–25). Here is a general summary of the exchange.

The crowds were continually around the Lord Jesus. They wanted signs, healings, and miracles. They were not concerned with him personally or his teachings—they simply wanted something from him. Of the crowds that searched after him, very few actually chose to follow him as his disciples. They just weren't interested in discipleship. They pursued him because they thought "the getting was good." On one occasion, however, a man broke from the crowd and "came to" the Lord Jesus because he knew the Lord was good. He even "ran up and knelt before" the Lord. He had a longing in his heart that he could not explain and did not know how to fulfill it. He asked the Lord a profound question: "Good Teacher, what must I do to inherit eternal life?"

Jesus did not usually receive questions like this in his public ministry. It was an inquiry that touched the very core of the Lord's saving mission. It revealed the integrity and spiritual depth of the man before him. And so, the Lord pushed back, "Why do you call me good? No one is good but God alone." In a rare disclosure, the Lord Jesus was willing to open the door for the man to see his divinity. But the revelation seemed lost on him. And so, the Lord gave him an answer to his question, namely, obey the commandments. Follow the moral law of the living God.

The man, who was "a ruler," was not satisfied with the answer and told the Lord, "Teacher, I have kept all these since my youth" . . . "what still do I lack?"

We are told the Lord Jesus looked at him, loved him, and said, "You lack one thing; go, sell what you own, and give the money to the poor, and you will have treasure in heaven; then come, follow me." The young ruler was told to abandon the idols of his heart. He was called out of the arena of false security and safety. He was invited to abandon his delusional convictions of his own radical autonomy. He was told to go and sell.

Such a command shows that the man's wealth and his abilities and talents—since he was no doubt some type of businessman with great means—needed to be given up for a good beyond himself. That was the form

of Jesus' personal invitation for this particular man to
follow him. Unlike the Galilean fishermen who readily
followed the Lord (Matt. 4:18–22), however, or Mathew
the tax-collector who abandoned his post to immediately (Matt. 9:9), the rich young man refused to give his
"yes" to Jesus. Instead, he was "shocked and went away
grieving."

In the early Church, life revolved around baptism and
faith, around the holy drowning and the repentance to a
personal decision for Jesus Christ. Such a foundation was
the impetus and means of perseverance in following the
way of the Lord.

Peter, the chief apostle, preached just this message on
the day of Pentecost:

> "Therefore let all Israel be assured of this: God
> has made this Jesus, whom you crucified, both
> Lord and Messiah."
>
> When the people heard this, they were cut to
> the heart and said to Peter and the other apostles,
> "Brothers, what shall we do?"
>
> Peter replied, "Repent and be baptized, every
> one of you, in the name of Jesus Christ for the
> forgiveness of your sins. And you will receive
> the gift of the Holy Spirit. The promise is for
> you and your children and for all who are far
> off—for all whom the Lord our God will call"
> (Acts 2:36–39).

This baptismal faith was the ground upon the early
Church was built and from which the gospel was proclaimed to the known world.

Have I surrendered all my possessions and talents to the Lord Jesus? Do I cling to anything other than the cross? Do I renew my personal decision for Jesus Christ every day and zealously do whatever he asks of me?

A Way of Life

The *baptismal way of life* is the way of the Lord. Following the Lord Jesus does not involve just a series of certain events or scattered acts but involves *everything* we do and *all* that we are.

Could you imagine if the Lord Jesus had attended the synagogue services and observed the annual worship in Jerusalem but did nothing else? Imagine the Lord reclining in his home, feet up, just taking it easy. Such an image does not parallel anything we see in the gospel about the life of the Lord. But imagine if that were how he lived. If he only observed worship "to get it out of the way" and then just chilled.

If people came to the Lord Jesus and asked about mercy, kindness, selfless service, and other such things, imagine him yawning and saying, "I'm really busy right now. The poor, sick, and suffering will have to take care of themselves." Or envision someone coming to him for fellowship and the Lord responding, "No, I'm good. There are a lot of things going on in my carpenter's shop. I don't have the energy for things like that." Or try to picture a group wanting to join him in prayer, only to have the Lord Jesus react in anger, "Prayer? I live in the real world. I can figure out my own problems. Prayer is for pious old ladies. I have to get things done."

If someone were to challenge the Lord on the above responses, could you ever even think that he would say something like, "Hey, back off, I make it to worship every week. I'm there for the Sabbath and religious festivals. That's enough!"

It's all ridiculous to imagine, of course. The Lord Jesus lived a way of life that fulfilled the prophetic vocation and reflected his love for God the Father and humanity. He was a man on a mission, and he lived a very specific way of life. Although liturgical worship was obviously the height of the Lord's life, it was not the only thing he did. Worship compelled a *way of life*.

It does for us, too. The oft-heard claim that we are "good Catholics" if we go to Mass on Sunday, notwithstanding how we neglect to follow the way of the Lord in the other areas of our lives, shows a severe misunderstanding of discipleship. We couldn't conceive of such a woefully minimalistic, self-manicured religiosity in the Lord's life. Why do we tolerate it in our lives—we who are called to imitate the Lord?

In observing the life and ministry of the Lord Jesus, we see his way and witness his singular devotion and obedience to the Father. The Lord tells us, "My food is to do the will of him who sent me and to complete his work" (John 4:34). He lived his entire life as an oblation to the Father and tirelessly and selflessly worked for our salvation. The pascal mystery was the culmination of a thirty-three-year life offered as an ongoing sacrifice. And so we have no excuses. The life we have received, the Lord also lived. And by his way of life, the Lord Jesus shows us what it means to be a child of God and how we are called to live and relentlessly work for him and his kingdom. The Lord has shown us his way and he calls us to follow him.

The Lord Jesus experienced all thing truly human (Heb. 4:15). He took on our nature and experienced all aspects of it as he sought to live his life as a libation. The

Lord felt hunger (Matt. 21:18) and thirst (John 19:28); he grieved (John 11:35), felt sorrow (Matt. 26:37–39) and disappointment (John 14:8–9); he experienced righteous anger (John 2:13–16), and he was troubled in spirit (John 13:21). The Lord underwent temptation (Matt. 4:1), felt pain and suffering (Matt. 16:21), and died (Matt. 27:50).

In each of these ways, he lived a human life, leaving us with no façades to hide behind, no rationalizations or justifications that hold water, and no defense to support holding back anything in following the way of the Lord.

In the gospel, we receive a glimpse of the Lord's determination, tenacity, and persistence. We are given a description of one day in his life (Luke 4:31–41; Mark 1:21–34). It was a day marked by worship and prayer, teaching, healing, exhortation, exorcisms, signs and wonders, eating, and holy fellowship. And early the next morning, after such a long day, the Lord Jesus departed to a deserted place and prayed (Luke 4:42). In this grace-filled and action-packed day, the Lord gives us an example of the days that we are called to live and offer to him. There is no slacking off, no recess, intermission, pauses, or time out. The way of the Lord includes our entire lives and calls for fervor, ardor, and a total devotion to him in all things.

Jesus invites us every day to come after him. His way is the way of sacrificial love. It is not an easy way. It is the path by which we follow the crucified and risen one and diligently work out our salvation.

Have I surrendered all the areas of my life to the lordship of Jesus Christ? Or have I created carve-outs and compromises to the demands of the Lord's way? Do I zealously and tirelessly offer up my life in total love and service to the Lord and his people?

A Way Unlike All Others

In the early ages of salvation history, when God called his servant Abraham to follow him, the patriarch did as he was asked. As the Lord God is rendering judgment against Sodom and Gomorrah for their grave sins, he says that Abraham was "chosen" to "keep the way of the Lord":

> Then the men set out from there, and they looked toward Sodom; and Abraham went with them to set them on their way. The Lord said, "Shall I hide from Abraham what I am about to do, seeing that Abraham shall become a great and mighty nation, and all the nations of the earth shall be blessed in him? No, for I have chosen him, that he may charge his children and his household after him to keep the way of the Lord by doing righteousness and justice; so that the Lord may bring about for Abraham what he has promised him" (Gen. 18:16–19).

The way of the Lord is not capricious or accidental. It is a *chosen* way. The Lord God calls his servants to follow it and his servants must obey and trust his way above all others.

The way of the Lord, as reflected in the life of Abraham and his descendants, was a way unlike all others. It was a way of "righteousness and justice." Although the servants of God were not always faithful to his way, the way was clear and its expectations were never dumbed down.

Later in salvation history, after 400 years of slavery in

Egypt, God ransomed his people and began the journey to bring them home to the Promised Land. The way of the Egyptians was different from the way of the Lord God and of their forefather Abraham. As God's people traveled and were purged in the desert, Moses interceded and asked God to "show me your ways." Moses realized that only the ways of the Lord could lead his people home.

> Moses said to the Lord, "See, you have said to me, 'Bring up this people'; but you have not let me know whom you will send with me. Yet you have said, 'I know you by name, and you have also found favor in my sight.' Now if I have found favor in your sight, show me your ways, so that I may know you and find favor in your sight. Consider too that this nation is your people" (Exod. 33:12–13).

As the forty years of purification in the desert concluded and God was about to welcome his people back into the Promised Land of Abraham, he called Moses—an old man near death—to remind and exhort his people. The ways of the Canaanites, who lived in the Promised Land, were wicked and idolatrous. As God's people entered the land, they needed to remain steadfast in the way of the Lord. The "path" of the Lord was given to them, and their hope and security could only be found "by walking in his ways."

> You must follow exactly the path that the LORD your God has commanded you, so that you may live, and that it may go well with you, and that you may live long in the land that you are to possess (Deut. 5:33).

> Therefore keep the commandments of the Lord your God, by walking in his ways and by fearing him. For the Lord your God is bringing you into a good land, a land with flowing streams, with springs and underground waters welling up in valleys and hills, a land of wheat and barley, of vines and fig trees and pomegranates, a land of olive trees and honey, a land where you may eat bread without scarcity, where you will lack nothing, a land whose stones are iron and from whose hills you may mine copper. You shall eat your fill and bless the Lord your God for the good land that he has given you. (Deut. 8:6–10).

Later in salvation history, when the time of the judges was coming to an end, God's people anticipated his actions and demanded a king. They told him,

> Then all the elders of Israel gathered together and came to Samuel at Ramah, and said to him, "You are old and your sons do not follow in your ways; appoint for us, then, a king to govern us, like other nations" (1 Sam. 8:4–5).

The way of the prophet Samuel was the way of the Lord, and the sons of Samuel rebelled against the way and offended God by their false worship and licentious behavior. In response, the elders insisted on having a king. This request for a king could have been a righteous one, except for the addition of "like other nations." The king of God's people is God himself. If he chose a king, the king would be his servant. He would serve God according to the covenant and law. The king of God's people would *never* be a king like the ones in the other nations.

As we saw in God's selection of David, the king of God's people would be uniquely God's own and shepherd in his name. He would follow God's way, which is distinct and superior to the ways of the nations. The king, like God's people themselves, was called to live in a different kind of life.

In his apostolic preaching, Paul attested to this peculiar vocation of King David (and all the faithful kings of God's people):

> When he had removed [Saul], he made David their king. In his testimony about him he said, "I have found David, son of Jesse, to be a man after my heart, who will carry out all my wishes" (Acts 13:22).

Although King David had his sins and struggles, he relished in the responsibility given to him as king. He celebrated God's way and called the people to follow it. Throughout the Psalms, which David wrote or collected, we see a steadfast summons to follow and rejoice in the way of the Lord:

> Teach me your way, O Lord,
>   and lead me on a level path
>   because of my enemies (Psalm 27:11).
> Happy are those whose way is blameless,
>   who walk in the law of the Lord.
> Happy are those who keep his decrees,
>   who seek him with their whole heart,
> who also do no wrong,
>   but walk in his ways (Psalm 119:1–3).

Throughout the prophetic writings, there is a strong and consistent beckoning to the way of the Lord. As the prophets pointed to the covenant of God, they taught, encouraged, corrected, and vehemently directed God's people back to the law of God and commanded them to adhere to the way of the Lord above all other ways.

The great prophet Isaiah called upon God's people to "prepare the way of the Lord":

> A voice cries out: "In the wilderness prepare the way of the Lord, make straight in the desert a highway for our God. Every valley shall be lifted up, and every mountain and hill be made low; the uneven ground shall become level, and the rough places a plain. Then the glory of the Lord shall be revealed, and all people shall see it together, for the mouth of the Lord has spoken" (Isa. 40:3–5).

The call to "prepare the way" was not the commissioning of a construction project, but a divine call to remove whatever blocked or hindered God's path to their hearts, so that the people could be prepared to recognize and welcome the Messiah when he came. The way of the Lord announced by Isaiah and the prophets was about spiritual dedication, moral rectitude, holy zeal for the majesty of God, a pining for his glory and a heartfelt obedience to his covenant.

Throughout salvation history the way of the Lord is laid before God's people. In the course of the ages, they are charged to remain faithful to it. This way, unlike all others, would distinguish them from the unbelievers, the idolaters, and the morally corrupt. This way, a pure gift from God, is the means by which they remain in a good relationship with the Lord.

It is no surprise, then, that Jesus would invoke the way of the Lord. In fact, he *identified* himself with it, declaring *himself* "the Way, the Truth, and the Life" (John 14:6). As the long-awaited anointed Savior, he *fulfilled* the way, just as he fulfilled every prophecy, promise, institution, event, and type in the Old Testament, culminating in his pascal mystery. He is the Way, and to follow the way of the Lord now means to follow him.

This fulfilled way of the Lord is now perfectly distinct from the way of unbelievers, sentimentalists, relativists, hedonists, and secularists. The way that smashed the false gods of the ancient world and exposed their poisonous and licentious ways is now the way that shatters the self-projected pet gods of today's pantheon. It lays waste the easy lies, the incomplete and erroneous anthropologies, the tyrannical rule of emotions, the delusional perceptions of reality, the moral relativism, and the hubris of modern civilization's god-makers. It is the way of the Power and Wisdom of God: supreme, sovereign, and sublime.

The way of the Lord makes us, today, unlike all other people. It separates us from the spiritual "other nations" of our world today. It is the way of "aliens and exiles," as Peter teaches us:

> Beloved, I urge you as aliens and exiles to abstain from the desires of the flesh that wage war against the soul. Conduct yourselves honorably among the Gentiles, so that, though they malign you as evildoers, they may see your honorable deeds and glorify God when he comes to judge (1 Pet. 2:11–12).

There is no compromise in the way of the Lord, no blending with other ways. It is the way of absolute truth.

It is also a challenging and arduous way. It compels us to trust in the Lord, to die to ourselves; and then, living for him, to rely constantly on the workings of his grace. It is the way of self-oblation and self-donation. It calls us to give everything we have. Yet it is worth this complete sacrifice, since it is the way that leads to true love, authentic happiness, and everlasting life. It is the path by which we journey with the Lord Jesus, who loved us and gave himself for us. It is the path by which we become fully who we are and were created to be: the children of God, brothers of the Lord Jesus, heirs of heaven. There is no equal, no competitor, no parallel to the way given to us by the living God. And so, we cling to the Lord Jesus and seek to faithfully and zealously follow his most excellent way.

Do I accept and live the demands of the Lord's way? Do I seek to look and live like "the other nations," such as my unbelieving neighbors, co-workers, and friends? Do I compromise my discipleship because I seek the respectability and esteem of others?

Signposts Along the Way

Years ago, in a conversation with a fallen-away Catholic, I inquired why the person left the Faith. Without batting an eye, she just looked at me—with a look that could kill—and responded, "Because being Catholic is not a way of life for respectable people." And that was it. She then walked away with nothing more to say.

Though I was saddened that the woman had left the way of the Lord, I was grateful for her candor and her perception. She's completely right: the way of the Lord is *not* for people who are concerned about the respectability and esteem of our fallen world and its elites. The Lord's way is a sign of contradiction (Luke 2:34–35). It reveals the hearts of many with its transparency, conviction, and authenticity, and is despised because of it.

Because the Lord's way is so distinct and unmistakable, there are "signposts" that clearly mark it and allow us to recognize it. Here are four of the most essential signposts along the way:

The first essential signpost of the Lord's way is *total and unconditional worship, devotion, and obedience* to the living and true God. The Lord's way vehemently and without apology denounces and distances itself from any and all forms of idolatry.

In the Christian life, there may be no sin greater than idolatry—when we replace the living God with a false god of our own imaginations. By our actions and affections we tell the one God, living and true, that we no longer believe in him or trust in him. We either abandon the true God or, just as often, we infect our devotion to him with attention to other deities of our own choosing. In the act of idolatry, we dethrone the one God from our hearts and replace him with variations of his own creatures or with projections we've created.

In selecting our own gods, we ultimately are only worshiping ourselves. We place ourselves upon the throne of our own hearts. In so doing, we usher in the chaos, dysfunction, and misery that come in a life without God. We turn the supernatural, relational, humble act of worship into a base, solitary, vain life of narcissism. Scripture compares the true worship of our relationship with God to the marital love between a man and a woman; idolatry, though, is like the lonely act of masturbation.

Idolatry is abhorrent to God, his majesty, and the loving kindness he shows to us from the sheer abundance of his goodness. There is no other offense or sin that can break the bond we have with God as severely or disastrously as idolatry. It is absolutely at odds with the Christian way.

The second essential signpost of the Lord's way is the *covenant*. It is imperative that we, as disciples of the Lord Jesus, understand what a covenant is and why it's at the heart of our interaction with the living God.

A covenant is a solemn, family-to-family agreement sealed by an oath. In a covenant, two become one; a larger family is formed. Covenants are usually made between equals. In his goodness, however, through the course of salvation history God has formed covenants with humanity. Each covenant ran its course in time and was fulfilled and expanded in the next covenant. God's first covenant with humanity was made at creation with Adam, our first earthly father. That covenant was fulfilled and taken into the covenant with Noah after the Flood, and then gave way to the covenant with our father Abraham. The Abrahamic covenant was completed and expanded by the covenant with Moses, which itself led to the covenant with King David.

Each covenant included further *revelations* from God, each covenant *broadened the base* of who was included in it, and each covenant deepened and enlarged God's blessings and promises to humanity. And each covenant was designed to prepare humanity and move it closer to the coming of the Messiah. When the Messiah came, he completed all other covenants and instituted a new, final, everlasting covenant.

> But Jesus has now obtained a more excellent ministry, and to that degree he is the mediator of a better covenant, which has been enacted

through better promises. For if that first covenant had been faultless, there would have been no need to look for a second one (Heb. 8:6).

The Messiah, the mediator of this ultimate covenant, is God himself. No one could have expected or anticipated such a gift! God *himself* would fulfill every promise, prophecy, event, institution, and type of the old covenants. God is Messiah. God is Lord and Savior.

He said to them, "But who do you say that I am?" Simon Peter answered, "You are the Messiah, the Son of the living God." And Jesus answered him, "Blessed are you, Simon son of Jonah! For flesh and blood has not revealed this to you, but my Father in heaven" (Matt. 16:15–17).

The New and Everlasting Covenant fully revealed God to the human family. In his Son, our Savior, God completes his project of loving self-disclosure to his people.

Long ago God spoke to our ancestors in many and various ways by the prophets, but in these last days he has spoken to us by a Son, whom he appointed heir of all things, through whom he also created the worlds. He is the reflection of God's glory and the exact imprint of God's very being, and he sustains all things by his powerful word. When he had made purification for sins, he sat down at the right hand of the Majesty on high, having become as much superior to angels as the name he has inherited is more excellent than theirs (Heb. 1:1–4).

The Lord Jesus has conquered the kingdom of sin and death and opened for us the way to eternal life. By his covenant, sealed by his pascal mystery—his passion, death, and resurrection—we are made adopted sons and daughters of God. The divine family is enlarged.

> For you did not receive a spirit of slavery to fall back into fear, but you have received a spirit of adoption. When we cry, "Abba! Father!" it is that very Spirit bearing witness with our spirit that we are children of God, and if children, then heirs, heirs of God and joint heirs with Christ—if, in fact, we suffer with him so that we may also be glorified with him (Rom. 8:15–17).

From the early Church until the end of time, every baptized person is sworn into the New and Everlasting Covenant. The baptized share in the work and promises of the covenant by exercising faith, making a personal decision for Jesus Christ, and faithfully following the way of our risen shepherd, earnestly working out our salvation in him.

> Now may the God of peace, who brought back from the dead our Lord Jesus, the great shepherd of the sheep, by the blood of the eternal covenant, make you complete in everything good so that you may do his will, working among us that which is pleasing in his sight, through Jesus Christ, to whom be the glory forever and ever. Amen (Heb. 13:20–21).

The third essential signpost of the way of the Lord is *our vocation to love*. The Lord Jesus explains this summons:

When the Pharisees heard that he had silenced
the Sadducees, they gathered together, and one
of them, a lawyer, asked him a question to test
him. "Teacher, which commandment in the law
is the greatest?" He said to him, "'You shall love
the Lord your God with all your heart, and with
all your soul, and with all your mind.' This is the
greatest and first commandment. And a second
is like it: 'You shall love your neighbor as yourself.' On these two commandments hang all the
law and the prophets" (Matt. 22:34–40).

As soon as we speak of love, however, we need to provide distinctions and clarifications. Sadly, the word has
been usurped and falsely or incompletely defined by our
culture. It is easy to misunderstand love or to use the
word to disguise our pride and ego.

In the Lord's way, love is about seeking the good of the
beloved. Love is not about us. Love is not about getting
something or feeling something. It is not reducible to eu-
phoria, arousal, pleasure, or consolation. The fallen world
tells us that love is about feelings of satisfaction or fulfillment. But real love, the love of Jesus' way, is not about
feeling filled-up but *pouring ourselves out* in self-donation
to our loved ones.

As in the early Church, so also today: we see love incarnate in the life and ministry of the Lord Jesus. We see
love crucified when we look upon the Lord hanging upon
the cross. We experience a clear and powerful "school of
love" in the Lord's passion, death, and resurrection.

St. John teaches us:

Beloved, let us love one another, because love is
from God; everyone who loves is born of God

and knows God. Whoever does not love does not know God, for God is love. God's love was revealed among us in this way: God sent his only Son into the world so that we might live through him. In this is love, not that we loved God but that he loved us and sent his Son to be the atoning sacrifice for our sins. Beloved, since God loved us so much, we also ought to love one another. No one has ever seen God; if we love one another, God lives in us, and his love is perfected in us (1 John 4:7–12).

We learn to love by witnessing the care, compassion, and selfless outpouring of the Lord Jesus for humanity. As he loves us, we are called to love him and one another. The early Church rallied behind the call of the Lord to love one another. The early disciples created a community of love and sought to share that love with the world around them. The early disciples sought to dynamically and compassionately live the Lord's exhortation, "By this everyone will know that you are my disciples, if you have love for one another" (John 13:35).

Accepting the mantle of love as a follower of the Lord's way, Paul gives us further teachings on love:

> If I speak in the tongues of mortals and of angels, but do not have love, I am a noisy gong or a clanging cymbal. And if I have prophetic powers, and understand all mysteries and all knowledge, and if I have all faith, so as to remove mountains, but do not have love, I am nothing. If I give away all my possessions, and if I hand over my body so that I may boast. but do not have love, I gain nothing.

> Love is patient; love is kind; love is not envious or boastful or arrogant or rude. It does not insist on its own way; it is not irritable or resentful; it does not rejoice in wrong-doing, but rejoices in the truth. It bears all things, believes all things, hopes all things, endures all things.
>
> Love never ends (1 Cor. 13:1–8a).

Unlike the pride, cruelty, violence, gossip, manipulation, lust, gluttony, impatience, rudeness, rash anger, perversion, greed, envy, deception, sloth, and all other vices that offend the Lord and objectify fellow human beings, the way of the Lord Jesus calls us to peace, patience, chastity, kindness, modesty, generosity, goodness, faithfulness, gentleness, self-control, and all other virtues that respect the Lord's commands and show respect for the value of every child of God. A love that appreciates all persons for themselves, and seeks to build up the good within them and to honor and protect their dignity, is a key signpost of the way.

The fourth essential signpost of the Lord's way is our summons to *mercy*. There is no clearer nor more countercultural action of the disciples of the Lord than the unreserved willingness to forgive and show mercy.

In the ancient world, life was brutal and unforgiving. God's revelations over the centuries instructed his people in the ways of mercy, culminating in the ultimate model of mercy in the life and death of the Lord Jesus. The early Christians sought to follow that model, and their mercy shined through the darkness of pagan barbarism. As the early Church did then, so now must Christians show themselves to be a people of mercy, in a world that is sliding back into ruthless cruelty.

As followers of the Lord's way, we ask for the desire to

live the Lord's beatitudes and so receive his blessings. We especially want to fulfill his summons to forgive: "Blessed are the merciful, for they will receive mercy" (Matt. 5:7).

The Lord Jesus lived mercy, showing it generously throughout his life. Even as he died upon the cross, he prayed for mercy: "Then Jesus said, 'Father, forgive them; for they do not know what they are doing'" (Luke 23:34).

When asked about mercy by Peter, the chief apostle, the Lord Jesus gave a startling and definitive answer:

> Then Peter came and said to him, "Lord, if another member of the church sins against me, how often should I forgive? As many as seven times?" Jesus said to him, "Not seven times, but, I tell you, seventy-seven times" (Matt. 18:21–22).

Throughout his teaching ministry, the Lord Jesus provided provocative and compelling parables about mercy. Such parables included the highly popular parables of the Prodigal Son (Luke 15:11–32), the Unforgiving Servant (Matt. 18:23–35), and the Publican and the Pharisee (Luke 18:9–14).

In the very early Church, Jesus' disciples responded to the summons to mercy by forgiving their tormentors and persecutors. Even as the early Christians were mocked, tortured, beheaded, crucified, thrown to wild beasts, and used as human torches, they heroically echoed the cry of the Lord Jesus: *Forgive them, for they know not what they do.*

Such mercy was a non-negotiable for those Christians. It was a blazing sign of their commitment to Jesus Christ and his gospel.

Paul was a special recipient of God's mercy, as he recounts:

I am grateful to Christ Jesus our Lord, who has strengthened me, because he judged me faithful and appointed me to his service, even though I was formerly a blasphemer, a persecutor, and a man of violence. But I received mercy because I had acted ignorantly in unbelief, and the grace of our Lord overflowed for me with the faith and love that are in Christ Jesus. The saying is sure and worthy of full acceptance, that Christ Jesus came into the world to save sinners— of whom I am the foremost. But for that very reason I received mercy, so that in me, as the foremost, Jesus Christ might display the utmost patience, making me an example to those who would come to believe in him for eternal life. To the King of the ages, immortal, invisible, the only God, be honor and glory forever and ever. Amen (1 Tim. 1:12–17).

As he had received mercy, he was keenly aware of his responsibility to give mercy. The apostle calls us, also, to be ministers of God's mercy and compassion:

So we are ambassadors for Christ, since God is making his appeal through us; we entreat you on behalf of Christ, be reconciled to God. For our sake he made him to be sin who knew no sin, so that in him we might become the righteousness of God (2 Cor. 5:20–21).

Finally, let us remember that the call to mercy is the Lord's command, but it is not a mere duty or chore. Indeed, it is a call to *freedom*. It is an invitation to *joy*. It is an opportunity to express *gratitude*. It lies at the very heart of the Lord's way, and so it directs us ultimately to happiness.

There are many other signposts along the way of the Lord, and as we journey on that way we will come to recognize them. But these four address its most essential aspects: the core of our relationship with the Lord Jesus and how we are to faithfully follow him. They show the way of true worship, familial covenant, selfless love, and generous mercy.

Do I avoid the veiled and deceptive forms of idols in the contemporary world? Do I give thanks for the opportunity to be a member of God's own family? Do I seek to selflessly love and serve others in the name of the Lord? Do I show generous mercy to those who have hurt or offended me or my loved ones?

The Final Conclusion of the Way

Earlier in my life, I was able to visit Nigeria. The archbishop who hosted me told me that I would leave Nigeria "more Catholic" than when I arrived there. And he was completely right, in many areas of discipleship. A renewed awareness and initiated hope for the Lord's glorious return was one of them. At the time I arrived, I knew and casually believed in the Lord's return, but it really wasn't something on my radar or something that I hoped for and prepared myself for every day.

Praying with the believers of Nigeria, watching their raised hands and listening to the shouts of "maranatha," "hosanna," "come, Lord," and "we wait for you," was emotionally moving and spiritually provocative. It was clear to me: these people are *truly waiting* for the Lord. They are calling out to him, joyful expectant of his return. Amid the poverty, governmental corruption, illnesses, sufferings, and other difficulties of their life, the believers of Nigeria still called out, "Your kingdom come!" They opened their hearts, exposed their vulnerabilities, poured themselves out in total supplication, and implored and petitioned the Lord Jesus every day to come that day.

The experience unsettled my comfortable Western belief in the Second Coming. In the course of days, as I began to care less about my composure and respectability and more about wanting the Lord to come and claim his victory, I began to pray with the body of believers. I was raising my own hands, calling out vocally—as I had never done before—"Lord, come now! I wait for you!" As I prayed in such a way, I was surprised to find myself shedding tears and weeping for the Lord's return. For the first time in my discipleship, I truly wanted the Lord to come. It was a completely transformative experience that changed my entire understanding of a doctrine I thought I had fully grasped.

During the Communion Rite of the sacred liturgy, as we prepare to receive a foretaste of heaven in the reception of the Lord's body and blood, we pray,

> Deliver us, Lord, we pray, from every evil, graciously grant peace in our days, that, by the help of your mercy, we may be always free from sin and safe from all distress, as we await the blessed hope and the coming of our Savior, Jesus Christ.

These are not meant to be empty words. We are *summoned as disciples* to "await the blessed hope and the coming of our Savior."

The truth of the Second Coming teaches us that there

will be an end to time and space. The Lord Jesus will return in glory and claim his victory. The early Church yearned and craved for the Lord's glorious return. They lived each day in joyful hope that the Jesus would return that day. Everything they did was oriented and arranged according to the acute realization that the Lord would return. The Second Coming was thus the exalted conclusion of the way of the Lord.

For too many Catholics today, though, the Second Coming has been effectively dismissed as a far-off fantasy—something not pertinent to our discipleship at this moment. The early Christians would not have understood such a lackadaisical and dismissive approach to the Lord's glorious return: the culmination of his saving work, the grand finale in which he will complete his victory over sin and death and present his kingdom to the Father. It will be the conclusion of the Lord's way and the encapsulation of all our hopes in him; how could we possibly have lost sight of that?

If indeed we do not hanker and hunger for the Lord's glorious return, the way of the Lord loses its prize and our discipleship is drained of its vitality. For, whether he is to return today or tomorrow, or in some future generation, our yearning for it is itself a cooperation with grace and a nurturing in hope that enlivens our souls and places our entire self in the hands of our Savior and Lord. Our fervent anticipation of the Second Coming allows the Lord *even now* to heal us, lift us up, and work out his salvation in us as we follow his way amid a fallen world.

By understanding the Second Coming as the ultimate conclusion of the way of the Lord Jesus, we are better able to realize and appreciate the supernatural perspective of the Lord's way. Oftentimes, even people of good faith and virtue can approach the way of the Lord as merely a temporal reality, something for this world only. But, by having a supernatural perspective grounded in the Second Coming, we are reminded of it and other related eternal truths, such as our particular death and judgment, purgatory, heaven, and hell.

Do I actively await the return of the Lord? Do I place our journey on the way of the Lord within a vigorous hope for his return? Do I earnestly prepare for eternal life with the Lord Jesus?

The Way to Eternal Salvation

A few years ago, I was driving through west Texas and New Mexico with a priest friend. The area is predominantly desert, so when a gas station says, "Last stop for 100 miles," it's not a joke. Neither of us had driven in that part of the country before and, needless to say, it was quite the adventure. On one occasion, the wind was getting strong, and the sand kept blowing onto the road—which was literally just some asphalt strewn through an arid strip of nothing. With the sand moving so quickly, it was hard to see the road since the sand would cover the road and disguise it.

If a car veered off the road and ended up stuck in the desert, it could be life or death (especially for two drivers who didn't know how to prep a car for such a road). The task of deciphering where the road was and staying on it was a full-time affair. We had to be alert and pay attention for the sake of our lives.

That memory comes to mind now, reminding us of the tenuous nature of staying on the way of the Lord. There is a lot of spiritual sand in our lives: obscuring the way, slowing our progress, and posing as an easier path. In order for us to remain on the true way of the Lord, we need to stay sober and alert (Matt. 24:42–44; Luke 21:36; 1 Pet. 5:8–9). We need to keep the destination always in sight. We need to be on guard against swirling mirages that *look* like the way but aren't.

The early Christians understood the need for such attentiveness along the way of salvation. Paul exhorted the Christians in Philippi,

> Therefore, my beloved, just as you have always obeyed me, not only in my presence, but much more now in my absence, work out your own salvation with fear and trembling; for it is God who is at work in you, enabling you both to will and to work for his good pleasure (Phil. 2:12–13).

The way of the Lord Jesus is a "hard road" both because it is marked by self-sacrifice and because it is not shifting sand but the sure, durable path under our feet. It is the means by which the Lord Jesus makes us fit for the kingdom of heaven. The way of the Lord is not just a path "that leads to life"—it is the *only* path that guides us into eternal life. In a fallen world and with our fallen hearts, the Lord's way is the sure way to guard and protect the fragile gift of our salvation in Jesus Christ.

Our life has only one of two ends: eternal life with Jesus Christ or eternal damnation with the Evil One. There is no middle ground, no compromised position, no neutral or safe space. There is no supposed "better place." There is only heaven or hell. We choose by the way of life we live and follow where we will spend eternity.

> Enter through the narrow gate; for the gate is
> wide and the road is easy that leads to destruc-
> tion, and there are many who take it. For the gate
> is narrow and the road is hard that leads to life,
> and there are few who find it (Matt. 7:13–14).

The early Christians understood and lived by this understanding of eternity, but today there are some who try
to circumvent the way of the Lord. They lie and convince
themselves that everyone—no matter what they do—is
going to heaven. They falsely believe that the only thing
someone needs to do to get to heaven is die! But this is
a total denial of the teachings of the Lord Jesus and his
stern and consistent call to be vigilant, alert, prepared,
and ready for judgment.

We have to be aware and discard the presumption of our
age. Our fallen nature has its consequences. Not everyone
who thinks about God, or calls upon him, or who does
some random work in his name, will merit eternal life.

> Not everyone who says to me, "Lord, Lord,"
> will enter the kingdom of heaven, but only the
> one who does the will of my Father in heaven.
> On that day many will say to me, "Lord, Lord,
> did we not prophesy in your name, and cast out
> demons in your name, and do many deeds of
> power in your name?" Then I will declare to
> them, "I never knew you; go away from me, you
> evildoers" (Matt. 7:21–23).

Whether we like it or not, we will stand in judgment.
There will be an accounting of our lives.

> When the Son of Man comes in his glory, and all
> the angels with him, then he will sit on the throne
> of his glory. All the nations will be gathered be-
> fore him, and he will separate people one from
> another as a shepherd separates the sheep from
> the goats, and he will put the sheep at his right
> hand and the goats at the left (Matt. 25:31–33).

The Lord desires the salvation of all. Heaven is open to
us in Jesus Christ.

> Then the king will say to those at his right hand,
> "Come, you that are blessed by my Father, in-
> herit the kingdom prepared for you from the
> foundation of the world; for I was hungry and
> you gave me food, I was thirsty and you gave
> me something to drink, I was a stranger and you
> welcomed me, I was naked and you gave me
> clothing, I was sick and you took care of me,
> I was in prison and you visited me." Then the
> righteous will answer him, "Lord, when was it
> that we saw you hungry and gave you food, or
> thirsty and gave you something to drink? And
> when was it that we saw you a stranger and
> welcomed you, or naked and gave you cloth-
> ing? And when was it that we saw you sick or
> in prison and visited you?" And the king will
> answer them, "Truly I tell you, just as you did it
> to one of the least of these who are members of
> my family, you did it to me" (Matt. 25:34–40).

As much as it might unsettle us, hell is real. The Lord

came to save us from its torments; and yet we are able to discard the gift of salvation and go to hell.

> Then he will say to those at his left hand, "You that are accursed, depart from me into the eternal fire prepared for the devil and his angels; for I was hungry and you gave me no food, I was thirsty and you gave me nothing to drink, I was a stranger and you did not welcome me, naked and you did not give me clothing, sick and in prison and you did not visit me." Then they also will answer, "Lord, when was it that we saw you hungry or thirsty or a stranger or naked or sick or in prison, and did not take care of you?" Then he will answer them, "Truly I tell you, just as you did not do it to one of the least of these, you did not do it to me." And these will go away into eternal punishment, but the righteous into eternal life (Matt. 25:41–46).

Hell is a place of utter horror and despair. It is a place devoid of love. It is a place of eternal displacement, of loneliness.

The Lord Jesus spoke more about hell than any other person in the entire Bible. He spoke more about hell than heaven, in fact, and his teachings on hell were graphic and evocative. He tells us that hell is a state of weeping and gnashing of teeth (Matt. 13:42), a place of outer darkness (Matt. 25:30), an unquenchable fire (Mark 9:43), an eternal torment (Luke 16:23), and a place of no return (Luke 16:19–31). The Lord Jesus also refers to hell as *Gehenna*, which was the place outside of Jerusalem with a wretched stench where garbage and trash were burned (Matt. 10:38).

The Lord Jesus tells us, "I watched Satan fall from heaven like a flash of lightning" (Luke 10:18). The Lord was present when hell was created for the fallen angels. He saw the dread and the barrenness of the place. He desires for none of God's children to go to such a horrible place. And so, he has come to us as the Messiah, the anointed Savior, to redeem us from sin and so ransom us from the evils of hell.

The way of the Lord is the path of redemption. It is the path of love and happiness. It is the only way to our salvation.

Do I realize the fragility of my salvation? Do I faithfully follow the way of the Lord and work out my salvation in Jesus Christ? Do I place all my words and deeds within the perspective of judgment and the realities of heaven and hell?

Application to Our Lives

Declarations of Discipleship

- I acknowledge the way of the Lord Jesus and seek to faithfully follow it.

- I believe in the transformative power of baptism and seek to fan its graces into flame within me.

- I declare Jesus Christ my Lord, Savior, and friend.

- I acknowledge the realty of heaven and hell and will orient my entire life to be made fit to be with God forever in heaven.

Examination of Conscience

The following questions are meant as a help in examining our own consciences on the way of the Lord.

- Have I personally and publicly declared Jesus Christ as the Lord of my life?

- Have I chosen to follow the way of the Lord in all I say and do?

- Do I live by a false or compromised way of life?

- Do I labor and work hard for the kingdom of God?

- Do I honor the gift of my baptism and seek to live by its grace?

- Do I regularly renew my baptismal promises?

- Do I adhere to the covenant of God and avoid all forms and variations of idolatry?

- Do I work to be an instrument of God's love to others?

- Do I generously show mercy to those around me?

- Have I refused to accept the realities of heaven and hell?

Having made this examination of conscience, go and make a good confession based on these points.

Key Points

As a help in speaking to our fellow believers and to unbelievers around us, here are some pointers for apologetics:

1. The Lord Jesus offers us his friendship. Biblically, friendship is synonymous with being a person's brother or an adopted member of a family.

2. Baptism is when we enter into the Lord's friendship. In baptism, we are called to live for the Lord Jesus and so die to ourselves.

3. In baptism, we re-live the pascal mystery of the Lord Jesus in our own lives.

4. The Lord calls us to follow his way, which includes our whole lives as we work out our salvation in him.

5. The way of the Lord is the way of the cross.

6. There are many false ways of life that do not compare with the way of the Lord.

7. We are invited to renew our dedication to the Lord by regularly renewing our baptismal promises.

8. The way of the Lord avoids idolatry, honors God's covenant, loves selflessly, and gives mercy generously.

9. Heaven and hell are real, and people go there forever.

10. The way of the Lord Jesus is not optional. It is the only way to eternal life in heaven.

Devotional Exercise

Act of Love

O my God, I love you above all things with my whole heart and soul, because you are all good and worthy of all my love. I love my neighbor as myself for the love of you. I forgive all who have injured me and I ask pardon of those whom I have injured. Amen.

The Mission of My Life (St. John Henry Newman)

God has created me to do him some definite service. He has committed some work to me which he has not committed to another. I have my mission. I may never know it in this life, but I shall be told it in the next. I am a link in a chain, a bond of connection between persons. He has not created me for naught. I shall do good; I shall do his work. I shall be an angel of peace, a preacher of truth in my own place, while not intending it if I do but keep his commandments. Therefore, I will trust him, whatever I am, I can never be thrown away. If I am in sickness, my sickness may serve him, in perplexity, my perplexity may serve him. If I am in sorrow, my sorrow may serve him. He does nothing in vain. He knows what he is about. He may take away my friends. He may throw me among strangers. He may make me feel desolate, make my

spirits sink, hide my future from me. Still, he
knows what he is about.

Suscipe

Take, Lord, and receive all my liberty,
my memory, my understanding,
and my entire will,
All I have and call my own.
You have given all to me.
To you, Lord, I return it.
Everything is yours; do with it what you will.
Give me only your love and your grace,
that is enough for me.
Amen.

Stations of the Cross

As you pray the stations of the cross, ask for the graces to
accept your cross and faithfully walk the way of the Lord
Jesus. In particular, focus on the *second station,* in which
Jesus accepts his cross: "So they took Jesus, and he went
out, bearing his own cross, to the place called the place of
a skull, which is called in Hebrew Golgotha" (John 19:17).

Rosary Suggestions

When praying the mysteries of the rosary, consider these
points:

Joyful Mysteries: The willingness of the Holy Family to
   follow the way of the living God.

Luminous Mysteries: The life of the Lord Jesus as a living
   sacrifice and oblation to the will of the Father out of
   love for him and for each of us.

Sorrowful Mysteries: The desire of the Lord Jesus to accept pain, suffering, and rejection as he walked the most excellent way of love.

Glorious Mysteries: The glory that awaits those who love God.

CHAPTER FOUR

THE EUCHARISTIC SACRIFICE, NOT A SYMBOLIC MEAL

For a day in your courts is better
than a thousand elsewhere.
I would rather be a doorkeeper in the house of my God
than live in the tents of wickedness.

—PSALM 84:10

Throughout my ministry, I have looked for mentors who can help me become a better Christian, priest, and pastor. One such mentor was a priest-academic who was always writing something and regularly involved in multiple projects.

On one occasion he shared with me the account of a Jewish rabbi that he had gotten to know. They were together working on a project involving the prophet Isaiah and the book of Psalms. They had been moving along in their research when the rabbi's adult daughter, his only child, was in a severe car crash and lost her life. The rabbi was thrown into a deep depression, and their project came to a halt.

Some months later, however, the rabbi reached out to the priest and asked if they could meet. When the two met up over coffee, the rabbi engaged in small talk and then, breathing heavily, he said to the priest, "I need to ask you to do something for me. Please don't overreact or read anything into it. It's been on my heart, and I need to ask you."

The priest was immediately humbled and said, "Of course, I'll do whatever I can. What do you need?"

The rabbi continued, "Could you please offer a Mass for my late daughter?"

The priest was understandably shocked by the request, but quickly responded, "Yes, I'd be honored to. Of course . . . May I ask . . . you're a Jewish rabbi and your daughter was Jewish. I'm happy to offer a Mass for anyone, but may I ask *why* you'd like a Mass for your daughter?"

In response, the rabbi sighed and said, "Yes, I'm Jewish, and that's not going to change. But I know that there is no greater worship than sacrifice. And I want the highest worship for my daughter. But I don't have a sacrifice to offer. You Christians, however—you do have a sacrifice. Could you please offer the sacrifice for my daughter?"

There was silence and then the priest spoke, "My God, you have an understanding of the Mass that most Christians don't understand. Yes, of course, without question, I will offer the holy sacrifice of the Mass for your daughter." And he did, with the rabbi present.

Our worship is indeed a *sacrifice*. It is the fulfilled Jewish sacrifice of Passover, in fact, by which Jesus Christ, "our paschal lamb," frees us from the slavery of sin and death. St. Paul taught the early Christians, and teaches each of us today,

> Your boasting is not a good thing. Do you not know that a little yeast leavens the whole batch of dough? Clean out the old yeast so that you may be a new batch, as you really are unleavened. For our paschal lamb, Christ, has been sacrificed. Therefore, let us celebrate the festival, not with the old yeast, the yeast of malice and evil, but with the unleavened bread of sincerity and truth (1 Cor. 5:6–8).

Worship is thus the heart of the Lord's way. It is the means by which we are presented to God and receive the grace we need to carry our cross and work out our salvation in Jesus Christ.

In the early Church, as Gentile Christians were being welcomed into the covenant of God, Paul boasted of his "priestly service" that allows "the offering of the Gentiles" to be acceptable and sanctified by God:

> I myself feel confident about you, my brothers and sisters, that you yourselves are full of goodness, filled with all knowledge, and able to instruct one another. Nevertheless on some points I have written to you rather boldly by way of reminder, because of the grace given me by God to be a minister of Christ Jesus to the Gentiles in the priestly service of the gospel of God, so that the offering of the Gentiles may be acceptable, sanctified by the Holy Spirit. In Christ Jesus, then, I have reason to boast of my work for God (Rom. 15:14–17).

The New Passover, the *Parousia* (presence), the Eucharist (thanksgiving): these are all early Christian names for the singular act of Christian worship, which is a sacrifice. The eucharistic sacrifice is the one sacrifice of Jesus Christ continually made present again for the sake of the baptized of every age until the Lord Jesus returns in glory.

Do I approach the Mass as a sacrifice? Do I realize that at Mass I am present at Calvary? Do I honor this holy sacrifice as the heart of my discipleship?

The Pascal Mystery and Eucharistic Sacrifice

The Lord Jesus came among us to redeem us. He lived his life as a continual oblation to the Father, and his living sacrifice culminated and was completed in his pascal mystery—the infinitely superior offering in which every sacrifice of the Old Covenant was fulfilled. The offering is the new manna (Exod. 16:4–36; John 6:31–63) that feeds God's people and gives them eternal life. It is the New Passover in which God definitively ransoms his people. It is the Bread of the Presence of the eternal Temple made flesh and dwelling in the midst of God's people.

The author to the Letter to the Hebrews beautifully describes the eucharistic sacrifice in a way steeped in Old Covenant imagery and meaning:

> But you have come to Mount Zion and to the city of the living God, the heavenly Jerusalem, and to innumerable angels in festal gathering, and to the assembly of the firstborn who are enrolled in heaven, and to God the judge of all, and to the spirits of the righteous made perfect,

and to Jesus, the mediator of a new covenant, and to the sprinkled blood that speaks a better word than the blood of Abel (Heb. 12:22–24).

The pascal mystery is the recapitulation of all God's words and deeds in Jesus Christ. It is the Lord's ultimate and complete scattering of darkness, vanquishing of sin, and defeating of death. The pascal mystery is the "sacrifice of atonement" by the blood of Jesus Christ. It is the overflowing of God's mercy and the opening of the doors of redemption and eternal life to all people in Jesus Christ.

But now, apart from law, the righteousness of God has been disclosed, and is attested by the law and the prophets, the righteousness of God through faith in Jesus Christ for all who believe. For there is no distinction, since all have sinned and fall short of the glory of God; they are now justified by his grace as a gift, through the redemption that is in Christ Jesus, whom God put forward as a sacrifice of atonement by his blood, effective through faith. He did this to show his righteousness, because in his divine forbearance he had passed over the sins previously committed; it was to prove at the present time that he himself is righteous and that he justifies the one who has faith in Jesus (Rom. 3:21–26) .

The pascal mystery *is* the eucharistic sacrifice, and the eucharistic sacrifice *is* the pascal mystery. The *Catechism* puts it succinctly: "The sacrifice of Christ and the sacrifice of the Eucharist are one single sacrifice" (1367).

The eucharistic sacrifice is thus not a mere nostalgic

recollection or an experience of spiritual sentimentalism. It the making-present of the pascal mystery in every age for the continuance of the Lord's saving mission until he returns in glory. The eucharistic sacrifice is the Holy Spirit re-presenting the passion, death, and resurrection of the Lord Jesus to the baptized of every generation. It is the *core* and *compass* of the Lord's way; or, what the Church calls the *source* and the *summit* of the entire Christian life.

The Second Vatican Council's teaching on the liturgy, *Sacrosanctum Concilium,* teaches us that

> the liturgy is the summit toward which the activity of the Church is directed; at the same time it is the font from which all her power flows. For the aim and object of apostolic works is that all who are made sons of God by faith and baptism should come together to praise God in the midst of his Church, to take part in the sacrifice, and to eat the Lord's Supper (10).
>
> At the Last Supper, on the night when he was betrayed, our Savior instituted the eucharistic sacrifice of his body and blood. He did this in order to perpetuate the sacrifice of the cross throughout the centuries until he should come again, and so to entrust to his beloved Spouse, the Church, a memorial of his death and resurrection: a sacrament of love, a sign of unity, a bond of charity, a paschal banquet in which Christ is eaten, the mind is filled with grace, and a pledge of future glory is given to us (47).

From the pascal mystery, made present by the eucharistic sacrifice, believers receive the grace of God and share in his very life. The holy sacrifice is the sacred river from which the Church receives all the sacraments of the Lord. As the sacraments are spread throughout the natural course of human life, they give us the grace that transforms us and makes us fit to dwell with God for all eternity.

Do I recognize the Passover as the fulfillment of God's words and deeds throughout the Old Covenant and the holy sacrifice of the Mass as the fulfillment of the Passover in the New? When I am present at the eucharistic sacrifice, do I reverently, actively, and consciously participate in the sacrifice?

The Covenant and the Sacraments

In the Upper Room, as the Lord Jesus fulfilled the Passover and initiated his pascal mystery, he inaugurated the New and Everlasting Covenant. Each of the previous covenants—with Adam, Noah, Abraham, Moses and David—were consumed and consummated in the New and Everlasting Covenant.

> When the hour came, he took his place at the table, and the apostles with him. He said to them, "I have eagerly desired to eat this Passover with you before I suffer; for I tell you, I will not eat it until it is fulfilled in the kingdom of God." Then he took a cup, and after giving thanks he said, "Take this and divide it among yourselves; for I tell you that from now on I will not drink of the fruit of the vine until the kingdom of God comes." Then he took a loaf of bread, and when he had given thanks, he broke it and gave it to them, saying, "This is my body, which is given

for you. Do this in remembrance of me." And he
did the same with the cup after supper, saying,
"This cup that is poured out for you is the new
covenant in my blood" (Luke 22:14–20).

The New and Everlasting Covenant is the definitive
covenant of salvation history. All of humanity is offered
the full revelation of the true and living God and the
opportunity for eternal salvation in Jesus Christ. The
early Church understood and valued this covenant. Jewish Christians saw holy baptism as the new circumcision
(Rom. 2:29; Col. 2:11–12): the mark of a person's entrance in the covenant with God. For this reason, the old
circumcision was not required of Gentile Christians; that
mark of belonging to god was considered fulfilled and no
longer applied in the New Covenant of Jesus Christ (Acts
15; 1 Cor. 7:17–20). Paul goes so far as to say that the
Church, the body of the baptized, is "the circumcision"
(Phil. 3:3). In this expression, the apostle is figuratively
using the ancient rite of circumcision as a symbol of con-
secration to God and separation from the unbelievers and
applying it to the Christian community, whose baptism
and faith in Jesus Christ set them apart.

Since baptism brings us into the New and Everlasting
Covenant, there is an intimate connection between baptism and the sacrifice of the covenant. The two cannot
be separated. Baptism complements the eucharistic sacrifice, and the eucharistic sacrifice enables and enriches
holy baptism.

In the baptismal way of life, believers seek to die to
themselves and live for Jesus Christ. There is a re-living
of the Lord's passion, death, and resurrection in the life of
every baptized person. Believers who are faithful to the
Lord's way in their daily life can approach the eucharistic

sacrifice and see within it the very mystery they are living. As they undergo their own processes of passion, death, and resurrection—dying to sin, temptation, fear, and anxiety—they are able to relate and have a radical and supernatural share of and solidarity with the Lord's, re-presented in the eucharistic sacrifice.

In such a way, in the eucharistic sacrifice the baptized person is also able to offer himself to God the Father through, with, and in the Lord Jesus. The Holy Spirit raises up the baptized and unites them to the Lord as he makes his sacrifice. In every age, as the eucharistic sacrifice is offered, the baptized are summoned to make themselves an offering with the Lord. Paul exhorts us:

> I appeal to you therefore, brothers and sisters, by the mercies of God, to present your bodies as a living sacrifice, holy and acceptable to God, which is your spiritual worship. Do not be conformed to this world, but be transformed by the renewing of your minds, so that you may discern what is the will of God—what is good and acceptable and perfect (Rom. 12:1–2).

In these ways and numerous others, the eucharistic sacrifice is truly the heart of the believer encountering and being transformed by the heart of Jesus Christ.

This relationship between the baptismal way of life and the eucharistic sacrifice is seen in the early Christians' profound love and adoration for the Blessed Sacrament. It inspired the early martyrs—some of whom died protecting the Eucharist—to see their sufferings and deaths in eucharistic imagery. The way of the Lord Jesus is a paschal way of life. It is a baptismal way. It is a eucharistic way.

From the pascal mystery, and its re-presentation in the eucharistic sacrifice through the ages, the covenant of God is rooted in our hearts, and from it the other sacraments are given to us. Each of the sacraments thus has a share in and connection with the pascal mystery.

The waters of baptism are a death to self, in order to live in Christ. Confirmation is the completion of baptism, and in it the believer receives the fullness of God's Spirit. Holy matrimony, in which one baptized man and one baptized woman are joined together to live in mutual love for the working out of their salvation and that of their children, reflects the passion, death, and resurrection of the Lord Jesus within the selfless and steadfast bond of the couple as they seek to be faithful to their vocation. In holy orders, God calls a man to make himself a special oblation and so reflect the pascal mystery in his efforts to die to himself and live solely for God and his Church. Confession and the anointing of the sick are paschal sacraments in that they bring healing from brokenness and life from death.

From the covenant of God celebrated and ratified in the pascal mystery, the baptized are invited to approach the holy altar and eat the body and drink the blood of Jesus Christ. Wonder of wonders! Joy of all joys! To be welcomed to the sacred altar and commune with the Lord is a gift, a blessing, an immense bestowal of divine grace, that no human being can deserve on his own merits. Only the loving kindness and sheer goodness of God makes it possible.

For the disciple, then, the reception of Holy Communion is literally no picnic. It's not a potluck or covered dish, or any type of casual meal. There's nothing relaxed, informal, or easy-going about it. Anyone who approaches for Holy Communion should be keenly aware of the great magnitude and serious character of the gift being offered, and conscious of his own unworthiness to be present at such a sacrifice and to participate in such a banquet.

The reception of Holy Communion is, furthermore, a *solemn public act* by which a person shows that he is in union with the Lord Jesus and his Church.

Sometimes, when people leave the Church, they say things like, "I wasn't being fed." When I hear such a comment, it has become my custom to reply, "Oh, you were being fed. You just didn't like what was on the menu." Holy Communion literally feeds us with God. Everything else is worth the work.

In receiving the body of the Lord, we declare that we are a follower of the way of the Lord Jesus. If anyone breaks such union with the Lord and his Church—by grave sin, apostasy, doctrinal disobedience, or public scandal—such a person should abstain from the reception of Holy Communion, since such a reception would be a lie and a sacrilege to the eucharistic sacrifice. St. Paul stresses this point to the early Christians, and to each of us:

> Whoever, therefore, eats the bread or drinks the cup of the Lord in an unworthy manner will be answerable for the body and blood of the Lord. Examine yourselves, and only then eat of the bread and drink of the cup. For all who eat and drink without discerning the body, eat and drink judgment against themselves. For this reason many of you are weak and ill, and some have died. But if we judged ourselves, we would not be judged. But when we are judged by the Lord, we are disciplined so that we may not be condemned along with the world (1 Cor. 11:27–32).

The apostle saw no compromise when it came to the eucharistic sacrifice: receiving Communion declares union with the Church and faithfulness to the Lord. If union or faithfulness is lacking, this condition must be mended and healed before someone can receive Holy Communion. Those who still receive in an unworthy manner thereby "eat and drink judgment against themselves." Notice how, in addition to the condemnation of one's soul, the apostle also associated the unworthy reception of Holy Communion with physical sufferings and ailments. To receive Communion unworthily is to unleash on a person torment of both soul *and* body.

Do I revere and honor the New and Everlasting Covenant celebrated in the eucharistic sacrifice? Do I seek intentionally to live the pascal mystery in my daily life? Do I examine myself so as to receive Holy Communion in a worthy manner?

Sacrament Before a Document

As we explore the reality and power of the eucharistic sacrifice, we need to understand its relationship with sacred scriptures, the written word of God.

While I was a seminarian in Rome, my apostolate was to give tours of St. Peter's and other churches and holy places throughout the Eternal City. One of the highlights for me was the catacombs, especially the Catacomb of Priscilla. Tradition attests that St. Peter himself, bishop of Rome and the first pope, frequently visited the *domus,* the house church, that rested atop the catacombs.

Today, the Catacomb of Priscilla is one of the five catacombs open to the public, and it's the only one cared for and supervised by religious sisters: the good Sisters of St.

Benedict, who run the catacomb and have preserved the spiritual nature of the holy place.

On one occasion, I was walking and giving a tour of the catacomb to a group of students from an American Bible college. The group was intrigued by the images of the Blessed Virgin, the bishop presiding over the eucharistic sacrifice, the Old Testament figures such as Noah, Jonah, Susanna, and Daniel, and the depictions of the Lord Jesus as the Good Shepherd. They were further intrigued—or unsettled—by the crammed locating of Christian burial sites around the resting places of known martyrs, as the early Christians wanted to honor and stay close to the holy martyrs and so share in their reward before God. As the tour concluded, one student—expressing the dismay of most of the group—just stared at me and asked, "But . . . where is this in the Bible?!"

Although sincere, the question was oddly placed in light of where we were standing. The Catacomb of Priscilla is located under a villa of the ancient senatorial family of Acilius Glabrio, who was condemned to death as an "atheist"—the charge used for Christians. After his death, Acilius's wife Priscilla (from whom the catacomb receives its name) and his son St. Pudens continued to support the Church. St. Paul mentioned Pudens in his second letter to Timothy (4:21).

Peter is said to have used their villa as the headquarters for his ministry in the Eternal City, giving Christian instruction, celebrating the Eucharist, and administering baptism there. As the chief apostle taught and baptized at Priscilla's house, he would have been accompanied by his disciple and interpreter John Mark. It was John Mark who composed his notes from Peter's teaching, and such notes eventually became what we now call St. Mark's Gospel.

It's odd, therefore, to ask where the practices evinced by the images and drawings of the Catacomb of Priscilla are found in the Bible, since the community of that domus helped give us a portion of the Bible!

The story highlights the common but faulty presumption that the Bible must have effectively fallen from the sky or that was received intact by the People of God, who then immediately used it to direct discipleship and the formulation of the Church. As illustrated by the community at the Catacomb of Priscilla, it happened in reverse order. The Lord Jesus wrote nothing. He didn't commission his apostles to write anything. He called them to *follow his way*, to live as he lived. The first disciples understood that the Word became flesh, not a book. They took Jesus' call to heart (Acts 2:42), and from their striving to live and preserve Jesus's way came the handing-on of apostolic tradition and then the New Testament.

Paul would emphasize this handing-on of the Lord's way by oral proclamation when he taught,

> But how are they to call on one in whom they have not believed? And how are they to believe in one of whom they have never heard? And how are they to hear without someone to proclaim him? And how are they to proclaim him unless they are sent? As it is written, "How beautiful are the feet of those who bring good news!" But not all have obeyed the good news; for Isaiah says, "Lord, who has believed our message?" So faith comes from what is heard, and what is heard comes through the word of Christ (Rom. 10:14–17).

And when did such teaching and preaching predominantly happen? During the assemblies of the believers for the eucharistic sacrifice.

As portions of the oral tradition began to be written down, quoted, or interpreted in writing, the Church started to collect them and codify them. When written collections of the Lord's life and teachings were received or when letters were sent by an apostle, the Christians would hear such writings proclaimed during the gathering for eucharistic worship. We noted that eucharistic worship came to be known by names that included *New Covenant* and *New Testament,* and when such collections or letters were read during worship, the writings came to be referred to as the writings of the New Testament, since that's where they were heard and taught.

By the late second century or early third, the phrase came to refer to the canonized twenty-seven books in our New Testament (and the older scriptures would be called the *Old Testament*), but it would always have its eucharistic roots, reflect the birth of those books from the living oral tradition of the Christian community as proclaimed during worship. The Holy Spirit brought forth the Christian scriptures from the way of the Lord, which is a eucharistic way.

Realizing the dynamics of the Lord's way and the Bible has led biblical theologian Scott Hahn to coin the expression, "The New Testament was a sacrament before it was a document."

And so, we cannot understand the Lord's way without the eucharistic sacrifice, and vice-versa. We cannot understand the Bible without the eucharistic sacrifice, and vice-versa. More specifically, we cannot understand the biblical New Testament without the *liturgical* New Testament, and vice-versa.

The dynamism and interaction between the way, the word, and the sacrifice is beautifully depicted in the story of the disciples on their way to Emmaus (Luke 24:13–34). The two disciples were "on the way," and the Lord Jesus had begun to teach them using the spoken and written word; but they couldn't understand, *until he broke bread with them.* It was in the breaking of the bread, the re-presentation of the sacrifice, that they saw the Lord and understood.

As Pope Benedict XVI taught in his apostolic exhortation *Verbum Domini,*

> From these accounts it is clear that Scripture itself points us toward an appreciation of its own unbreakable bond with the Eucharist. "It can never be forgotten that the divine word, read and proclaimed by the Church, has as its one purpose the sacrifice of the new covenant and the banquet of grace, that is, the Eucharist." Word and Eucharist are so deeply bound together that we cannot understand one without the other: the word of God sacramentally takes flesh in the event of the Eucharist. The Eucharist opens us to an understanding of Scripture, just as Scripture for its part illumines and explains the mystery of the Eucharist. Unless we acknowledge the Lord's real presence in the Eucharist, our understanding of Scripture remains imperfect (55).

The written word of God, united with the oral tradition, is the sacred deposit of faith given to us by the Lord Jesus. From the New Covenant sacrifice, we receive the grace we need to hear, understand, and live by the truth and tenets of the catholic and apostolic faith.

Do I regularly read the Bible? Do I interpret and seek to understand the Bible in light of the eucharistic sacrifice? Do I make efforts to read and prepare myself for the biblical readings that are proclaimed during Sunday Mass?

Commandment and Commission

As the Lord Jesus concluded his public ministry, he offered his saving sacrifice and told his apostles to "do this in memory of me" (Luke 22:19–20). This command resonated throughout the early Church and was carried by the apostles and their priestly co-workers, and eventually their successors. Such widespread observance is made clear by the testimony of St. Paul, who sometime later recounted the Lord's command:

> For I received from the Lord what I also handed on to you, that the Lord Jesus on the night when he was betrayed took a loaf of bread, and when he had given thanks, he broke it and said, "This is my body that is for you. Do this in remembrance of me." In the same way he took the cup also, after supper, saying, "This cup is the new covenant in my blood. Do this, as often as you drink it, in remembrance of me." For as often as you eat this bread and drink the cup, you proclaim the Lord's death until he comes (1 Cor. 11:23–26).

In addition to the command, "Do this in memory of me," the Lord Jesus gave the Great Commission:

> Go therefore and make disciples of all nations, baptizing them in the name of the Father and of the Son and of the Holy Spirit, and teaching them to obey everything that I have commanded you. And remember, I am with you always, to the end of the age (Matt. 28:19–20).

The eucharistic command and the Great Commission are complementary directives from the Lord Jesus. As we celebrate the Eucharist, we must teach. As we go to teach, we must celebrate the Eucharist. The Church was evangelistic because it was eucharistic, and it was eucharistic because it was evangelistic.

In the Emmaus account, after the disciples saw the Lord Jesus in the breaking of the bread, they ran to Jerusalem—even though it was evening and the city was several miles away. They ran to announce the good news:

> That same hour they got up and returned to Jerusalem; and they found the eleven and their companions gathered together. They were saying, "The Lord has risen indeed, and he has appeared to Simon!" Then they told what had happened on the road, and how he had been made known to them in the breaking of the bread (Luke 24:33–35).

This close connection between sacrifice and mission has given rise to a newer name for the eucharistic sacrifice: the *Mass*. This term comes from the imperative at the conclusion of the sacred liturgy of the Roman Rite: "*Ite, missa est.*" The Latin here is actually tricky to translate. In essence, it means, "Go, it has concluded," or more casually, "It's over. Get out of here." In time, the whole liturgy took on the name "Mass" from that Latin word for sending-forth. As the *Catechism* explains, it is called

> *Holy Mass (Missa),* because the liturgy in which the mystery of salvation is accomplished concludes with the sending-forth (*missio*) of the faithful, so that they may fulfill God's will in their daily lives (1332).

In this very name, we see the merging of the eucharistic sacrifice with the Christian call to mission and evangelization. *This has been the eucharistic sacrifice. Go, preach the good news and bring the whole world to the eucharistic sacrifice.* Our worship feeds the mission of evangelization, and the mission of evangelization calls for the acknowledgement of the one true God and worthy worship of him in spirit and in truth.

Do I accept the eucharistic command and the Great Commission of the Lord Jesus? Do I participate in Mass with devotion and attentiveness? Do I share the gospel with those around me?

Application to Our Lives

Declarations of Discipleship

- I acknowledge the pascal mystery as the source of the New and Everlasting Covenant of Jesus Christ.

- I recognize the eucharistic sacrifice as the re-presentation of the pascal mystery and the sacrifice of the New Covenant for all ages.

- I accept my entrance into the New and Everlasting Covenant through baptism and will obey the Lord's command to participate in the eucharistic sacrifice and his commission to teach all nations.

Examination of Conscience

The following questions are meant as a help in examining our own consciences on the sacredness and importance of the Mass.

- Do I prepare for Sunday Mass and see it as the highlight of my entire week?

- Do I ensure that I'm in the state of grace for the Mass?

- Do I regularly go to Confession to live a life of grace?

- Do I show reverence during Mass and actively participate in the prayers?

- During Mass, do I offer myself with the Lord Jesus to the Father?

- Do I see my life as a participation in the pascal mystery?

- Do I reject or accept the passion that comes with temptation, fear, and anxiety?

- Do I regularly read the Bible?

- Do I allow the secular world to make me ashamed of my faith?

- Do I share the gospel with those around me?

Having made this examination of conscience, go and make a good confession based on these points.

Key Points

As a help in speaking to our fellow believers and to unbelievers around us, here are some pointers for apologetics:

1. The pascal mystery is the passion, death, and resurrection of Jesus Christ.

2. The pascal mystery is the culmination of all the words and deeds of God throughout salvation history.

3. The New and Everlasting Covenant is given to us through the pascal mystery.

4. The pascal mystery is re-presented (made present again) in the eucharistic sacrifice, also called the New Passover, the breaking of the bread, the New Covenant (Testament), and the Mass. This is not nostalgic recall or an experience of spiritual sentimentalism. It is the real and actual making-present of the Lord's pascal mystery.

5. The eucharistic sacrifice is the sacrifice of the New and Everlasting Covenant.

6. We enter the New Covenant through holy baptism.

7. All of the sacraments come to us through the pascal mystery.

8. We are called to receive the body and blood of the Lord in a worthy manner. To do otherwise would be to eat and drink judgment against ourselves.

9. There is a complementarity and dynamism between the Lord's way, the eucharistic sacrifice, and the sacred scriptures.

10. As baptized Christians, we are called to celebrate the eucharistic sacrifice and share the good news.

Devotional Exercise

Act of Spiritual Communion

My Jesus, I believe that you are in the Blessed Sacrament. I love you above all things, and I long for you in my soul. Since I cannot now receive you sacramentally, come at least spiritually into my heart. As though you have already come, I embrace you and unite myself entirely to you; never permit me to be separated from you.

The Angel's Prayer of Fatima

Most Holy Trinity—Father, Son and Holy Spirit—I adore thee profoundly. I offer you the most precious body, blood, soul and divinity of Jesus Christ, present in all the tabernacles of the world, in reparation for the outrages, sacrileges, and indifferences whereby he is offended. And through the infinite merits of his Most Sacred Heart and the Immaculate Heart of Mary, I beg of you the conversion of poor sinners.

Prayer Before Mass (St. Thomas Aquinas)

Almighty and everlasting God, behold I come to the sacrament of your only-begotten Son, our Lord Jesus Christ: I come as one infirm to the physician of life, as one unclean to the fountain of mercy, as one blind to the light of everlasting brightness, as one poor and needy to the Lord of heaven and earth. Therefore I implore the abundance of your measureless bounty that you would vouchsafe to heal my infirmity, wash my uncleanness, enlighten my blindness, enrich my poverty and clothe my nakedness, that I may receive the bread of angels, the king of kings, the Lord of lords, with such reverence and humility, with such sorrow and devotion, with such purity and faith, with such purpose and intention as may be profitable to my soul's salvation.

Grant unto me, I pray, the grace of receiving not only the sacrament of our Lord's body and blood, but also the grace and power of the sacrament. O most gracious God, grant me so to receive the body of your only-begotten Son, our Lord Jesus Christ, which he took from the Virgin Mary, as to merit to be incorporated into his mystical body, and to

be numbered among his members. O most
loving Father, give me grace to behold forever your beloved Son with his face at last
unveiled, whom I now purpose to receive
under the sacramental veil here below. Amen.

Stations of the Cross

As you pray the stations of the cross, ask for the graces
to revere the eucharistic sacrifice and avoid all sacrilege
or disrespect to the Lord. In particular, focus on the *first
station*, where Pilate dismisses the nobility of the Lord and
condemns him to death: "So when Pilate saw that he was
gaining nothing, but rather that a riot was beginning, he
took water and washed his hands before the crowd, saying, 'I am innocent of this righteous man's blood; see to
it yourselves'" (Matt. 27:24).

Rosary Suggestions

When praying the mysteries of the rosary, consider these
points:

Joyful Mysteries: The goodness of the Lord to come to us
and the sacredness of his body and soul.

Luminous Mysteries: The words and deeds of the Lord Jesus that are culminated and consummated in his pascal
mystery, which is re-presented to us at every Mass.

Sorrowful Mysteries: The horrific and sacrilegious treat-
ment of the body of the Lord Jesus during his passion,
as well as the ongoing sacrilege of the Eucharist by
many Christians.

Glorious Mysteries: The glory of the Lord's resurrected
body and soul, and our call to share in that glory with
him.

BE AN UNCOMPROMISED DISCIPLE!

Real discipleship is when we hear the call of the Lord Jesus to follow him and then strive, with all our efforts, to heed the call. The demands of discipleship can seem intimidating. This should lead us to the awareness of our need for God's help and the constant workings of his grace. We are fallen people, and, left to our own devices, we tend to accommodate discipleship to our own needs, wants, and comfort level—to be a *compromised* disciple.

The compromised disciple hears the summons of the Lord Jesus and sees the many demands of the Lord's way, and says, "Are you kidding me?!" The call to mercy and the forgiveness of our enemies—are you kidding me?! The expectation to pray often and to rely on divine wisdom to make the decisions of our lives—are you kidding me?! The teaching to accept the burdens of others and selflessly serve those in need—are you kidding me?! The summons to live simply and generously give to others—are you kidding me?!

To the compromised disciple, it sounds reasonable, enlightened, and mature to question the hard parts of Jesus' way, but it's actually irrational, endarkening, and juvenile, because it leaves no room to change or grow. It is fallen humanity's defense mechanism against unsettling challenges—including the graces of conversion. "Are you kidding me?!" is one of the greatest false creeds of our day.

Have I fallen into the "are you kidding me" mentality? Do I preserve a healthy suspicion of myself and pray often for objectivity? Do I allow grace to constantly challenge and unsettle me so that I can grow in the way of the Lord?

Shoulders of Giants

On the way of the Lord Jesus, we don't walk alone and we're not left to forge the path ourselves. No, we stand on the shoulders of giants. Our forebears in the faith, from the men and women who first followed the Lord Jesus to all his saintly disciples throughout the ages, have made the way clear and allow us to see past any obstacle. They offer us a powerful witness to the power and excellence of the Lord's way, and we can regularly turn to them and be inspired by their examples and assisted by their prayers.

Compared to such giants, we can look and feel like ants! In this book, we have examined the many errors that compromise discipleship in our day—secularism, relativism, sentimentality, selfishness—and we have noted how many people, including baptized Christians, think that a good life is one that is lived by their own wants and standards. None of us, however earnest our intentions, is immune to these influences and their temptation to compromise. The grace of God, however, is more powerful than all of them.

The first Christians had to overcome other obstacles and temptations to compromised discipleship, but they all tended toward the same self-centeredness. Over the centuries, the words and ideologies have changed, but the threat is the same! And yet, just as our forefathers and foremothers overcame those obstacles and lived holy and good lives, converting the Roman Empire and other pagan nations, so each of us in our day has the grace necessary to earnestly follow the way of the Lord Jesus, achieve holiness, and convert the nations of our day.

Our task is to avoid idolatry and cling to the one, true God, adhere without compromise to the full gospel of Jesus Christ, zealously follow his way of love, offer true worship in spirit and truth, and so work out our salvation in this life and dwell forever with God in heaven. This is the purpose of our lives. It's why we were created and why we have received the graces, talents, and vocations that we have in this life.

Have I falsely assumed that salvation is guaranteed to me? Have I given in to desolation and lost hope for conversion and a return to the Lord in myself and my nation? Do I understand why I have been created and so I seek above all things to work out my salvation in Jesus Christ?

A Prayer

As we conclude our teachings and reflections on real discipleship, let us direct our wills to humbling ourselves and giving everything to the Lord. Let us ask his blessing, entrusting our discipleship to him, without whom we cannot follow the way. The Lord's way calls for self-oblation and sacrifices, but its destination is worth all of them; as we hope for eternal life in Jesus Christ and renew our vow to remain true and steadfast to the Lord Jesus, let us conclude with the wisdom of St. Paul. With bowed heads, we prayerfully accept his exhortation and ask God for the graces of fidelity and perseverance.

> As for me, I am already being poured out as a
>   libation,
> and the time of my departure has come.
> I have fought the good fight,
> I have finished the race,
> I have kept the faith.
> From now on there is reserved for me the crown
>   of righteousness,
> which the Lord,
> the righteous judge,
> will give me on that day,
> and not only to me but also to all who have
>   longed for his appearing.
>
> —2 TIMOTHY 4:6–8

SUGGESTED READING FOR REAL DISCIPLES

Jesus Began to Preach: The Mystery of God's Word, by Raniero Cantalamessa. Collegeville, Pa.: Liturgical Press, 2010.

The Meaning of Tradition, by Yves Congar. San Francisco: Ignatius Press, 2004.

The Church of Apostles and Martyrs, Volumes I and II, by Henri Daniel-Rops. Providence: Cluny Books, 2022.

Living the Gospel Without Compromise, by Catherine Doherty. Combermere: Madonna House Publications, 2002.

Liturgical Dogmatic, by David Fagerberg. San Francisco: Ignatius Press, 2021.

Consuming the Word, by Scott Hahn. New York: Image Books, 2013.

Letter and Spirit, by Scott Hahn. New York: Doubleday, 2005.

Swear to God, by Scott Hahn. New York: Doubleday, 2004.

The Lamb's Supper, by Scott Hahn. New York: Doubleday, 1999.

Chance or the Dance? A Critique of Modern Secularism, by Thomas Howard. San Francisco: Ignatius Press, 2001.

At the Origins of Christian Worship, by Larry Hurtado. Grand Rapids, Mich.: Eerdmans Publishing, 1999.

Destroyer of the Gods: Early Christian Distinctiveness in the Roman World, by Larry Hurtado. Waco, Tex.: Baylor University Press, 2016.

Wedding Feast of the Lamb: Eucharistic Theology from a Biblical, Historical, Systematic Perspective, by Roch A. Kereszty. Chicago: Hillenbrand Books, 2004.

Glory Unto Glory: A Primer on Ascetical Theology, by Fr. Jeffrey Kirby. Brooklyn: Angelico Press, 2022.

Journey to Mount Carmel, by Fr. Jeffrey Kirby. Nashua, N.H.: Sophia Institute Press, 2022.

Lord, Teach Us to Pray: A Guide to the Spiritual Life and Christian Discipleship, by Fr. Jeffrey Kirby. Charlotte: St. Benedict Press, 2014.

The Way of the Disciple, by Erasmo Lieva-Merikakis. San Francisco: Ignatius Press, 2003.

The Idol of Our Age: How the Religion of Humanity Subverts Christianity, by Daniel Mahoney. New York: Encounter Books, 2018.

Jesus and the Jewish Roots of the Eucharist, by Brant Pitre. New York: Doubleday, 2011.

Jesus and the Last Supper, by Brant Pitre. Grand Rapids, Mich.: Eerdmans Publishing, 2015.

Introduction to Christianity by Card. Joseph Ratzinger. San Francisco: Ignatius Press, 2004.

Jesus of Nazareth: From the Baptism in the Jordan to the Transfiguration, by Card. Joseph Ratzinger. New York: Doubleday, 2007.

The God That Did Not Fail: How Religion Built and Sustains the West, by Robert Royal. New York: Encounter Books, 2010.

A Secular Age, by Charles Taylor. Cambridge: Belknap Press, 2007.

The Incredible Catholic Mass, by Martin Von Cochem. Charlotte, N.C.: TAN Books, 2012.

Forming Intentional Disciples, by Sherry Weddell. Huntington, Ind.: Our Sunday Visitor, 2012.

ABOUT THE AUTHOR

Father Jeffrey Kirby, S.T.D., is a Papal Missionary of Mercy, the Pastor of Our Lady of Grace Parish in Indian Land, South Carolina, and the Host of the daily devotional *Daily Discipleship with Father Kirby*. He holds a doctorate in moral theology from the University of the Holy Cross in Rome and serves as an adjunct professor of theology at Belmont Abbey College. He is the author of several books, including *Real Religion: How to Avoid False Faith and Worship God in Spirit and Truth*.